Honoring Identities

Honoring Identities

Creating Culturally Responsive Learning Communities

Donna L. Miller

ROWMAN & LITTLEFIELD
Lanham • Boulder • New York • London

Published by Rowman & Littlefield
A wholly owned subsidiary of The Rowman & Littlefield Publishing Group, Inc.
4501 Forbes Boulevard, Suite 200, Lanham, Maryland 20706
www.rowman.com

6 Tinworth Street, London SE11 5AL, United Kingdom

Copyright © 2021 by Donna L. Miller

All rights reserved. No part of this book may be reproduced in any form or by any electronic or mechanical means, including information storage and retrieval systems, without written permission from the publisher, except by a reviewer who may quote passages in a review.

British Library Cataloguing in Publication Information Available

Library of Congress Cataloging-in-Publication Data

Library of Congress Control Number: 2020946313
ISBN 978-1-4758-5787-0 (cloth)
ISBN 978-1-4758-5788-7 (paper)
ISBN 978-1-4758-5789-4 (electronic)

Contents

Foreword   vii

Preface   xi

Introduction: Finding Purpose   1

1   Cultural Identity   7

2   Building Community and Connections   15

3   Teacher and Student Dispositions   35

4   Nurturing Social Justice   49

5   The Power of Talk and Dialogic Exchange   75

6   Reading Cultural Identity Literature   93

7   Pause and Ponder Moments   123

Appendix: Annotated List of Cultural Identity Literature   141

References   153

Index   159

About the Author   163

Foreword

Beverly Ann Chin, PhD, Professor of English and Director of the English Teaching Program and the Montana Writing Project at the University of Montana, Missoula

Many teachers are concerned their students do not make personal connections as they read multicultural literature. Some students may resist this literature because they do not share the same ethnicity, race, or religion as the characters. Some students may not understand the characters' challenges because they come from different socioeconomic backgrounds or identify with a gender different from that of the characters. Teachers also worry when they hear students make comments that stereotype (either negatively or positively) the characters in multicultural literature and perhaps extend these overgeneralizations to their classmates and other people in the local and global society.

As literacy educators, we seek sound teaching strategies and quality literary texts that help students grow in their understanding of their own identities and culture as well as deepen their appreciation of other people's identities and cultures. Because all educators want students to mature as literate, respectful, and responsible people, I am delighted to introduce you to Donna Miller's *Honoring Identities*, a book that informs and inspires educators to teach multicultural texts—what she renames Cultural Identity Literature—in culturally responsive ways.

Based on over thirty years of teaching students of diverse backgrounds and abilities, Donna presents a multitude of successful strategies that engage students in interrogating culture and identity as they read literary texts, create community, and exchange perspectives. *Honoring Identities* helps literacy teachers expand and enrich their teaching of Cultural Identity Literature by providing both the theoretical framework and the practical application of the innovative learning tool, GREEN APPLE.

GREEN APPLE is an acronym that provides teachers with a comprehensive method for recalling key features of identity: **G**ender, **R**eligion, **E**thnicity and race, **E**conomic class/socioeconomic status, **N**ame/family, **A**ge, **P**lace (national territory/geography), **P**erception of belonging, **L**anguage, and **E**xceptionality (gifted or challenged).

As you read *Honoring Identities*, you will discover that this simple acronym is not simplistic. GREEN APPLE is a carefully constructed framework for investigating culture and identity as dynamic, multifaceted, complex concepts. By summarizing the current research on culturally responsive pedagogy and describing her on-going work with students and teachers, Donna Miller shows us the potential and power of GREEN APPLE.

In each chapter of *Honoring Identities*, Donna focuses on essential knowledge, skills, and dispositions for teaching students about culture and identity. She guides teachers in specific ways to build safe, inclusive learning communities; to structure thought-provoking classroom conversations; and to analyze negative and positive stereotypes. Above all, she asks teachers to pause and to ponder their own philosophy and classroom practices for teaching students about identity and culture.

By discussing her own experiences and providing excellent resources, Donna guides teachers in the application of the elements of GREEN APPLE to immerse students in the exploration and examination of cultural identity texts. First, GREEN APPLE can widen and deepen the selection of cultural identity texts for students at different grade levels and reading abilities, interests, and attitudes. Some texts might richly embody several of the GREEN APPLE features; other texts might focus deeply on only one or two features. Upon reviewing these multicultural texts, teachers can consider which selections are most appropriate for the whole class, small groups, and/or independent reading.

By using GREEN APPLE, teachers can re-read texts and reflect on their own understandings and questions about culture and identity. Teachers can also consider how students might respond to these cultural identity texts across genres. By consistently using GREEN APPLE as they select texts, teachers offer students a broader range of perspectives on the multidimensional concepts of identity and culture.

In addition to addressing the importance of purposeful text selection, GREEN APPLE provides a valuable framework for crafting essential questions and planning instructional activities for inquiry units on culture and identity. Teachers can naturally weave GREEN APPLE into culturally responsive strategies, such as discussion questions, writing prompts, journal entries, Socratic seminars, creative drama activities, multimedia projects, and multi-genre portfolios. Teachers can encourage students to examine their own and others' perceptions of identity and culture through all the language arts—reading, writing, speaking, listening, viewing, and visually representing.

By strategically using GREEN APPLE throughout the curriculum, teachers make explicit for students the dynamic interfaces of culture and identity. Teachers can model ethical behavior and respectful civil discourse as students explore sensitive issues of race, gender, religion, and socioeconomic status. When students learn GREEN APPLE as an inquiry lens, they gain agency, voice, and confidence in their own identities and cultures as they develop insights and empathy into the identities and cultures of others.

Honoring Identities offers all teachers a wealth of specific ways to integrate social justice, civil discourse, and equity in the classroom and curriculum. If you are new to the profession, this book supports you as you develop instructional activities; if you are experienced in teaching for social justice, this book encourages you to refine your repertoire of activities.

For years, I have celebrated Donna Miller as a highly accomplished literacy educator. Donna is widely respected as a classroom teacher, a college methods professor, and a teacher consultant and co-director in Writing Projects in Montana. At conferences and professional development sessions, teachers praise Donna's modeling of reading/writing workshops on culturally responsive pedagogy. Donna's passionate commitment to transformative teaching for social justice, diversity, and inclusion permeates her writing.

As you read *Honoring Identities*, you enjoy an intimate, professional conversation with an extraordinary educator. Donna welcomes all teachers into this authentic dialogue about teaching cultural identity literature. I know you will be excited to use GREEN APPLE with your students and to share this exceptionally valuable resource with your colleagues. *Honoring Identities* invites you to reflect honestly and empathetically on the intricate intersections of your own and your students' cultures and identities.

By using GREEN APPLE, you join a professional learning community dedicated to nurturing all students as critical readers, effective writers, reflective thinkers, and socially responsible, ethical community members.

Preface

In *Honoring Identities,* I argue that all students will benefit if we take the time to learn about one another. In classrooms that foster dialogic exchange, mutual respect, and an obligation to decency, students might experience a climate where individuals speak from a distinct perspective while remaining open to alternate perspectives.

While the book in your hands includes general knowledge held by many members of the educational community, it builds on those premises we hold in common and combines insight from multicultural education theory and from my thirty-eight years of intentional and systematic inquiry conducted in public secondary and post-secondary classrooms performed with the goal of gaining insights into teaching and learning.

Additionally, it borrows from the scholarship of multiple researchers for its rationality and justification, as well as from my many colleagues who shared teaching ideas at National Writing Project Summer Institutes, educator conferences, and professional development workshops. The GREEN APPLE questions that readers will encounter provide a framework for both discussing and selecting Cultural Identity Literature (CIL) and for reading ourselves and the world.

Reading CIL and conducting many of the activities outlined in *Honoring Identities* enables us all to learn from literature and scholarship that highlight the experiences of multiethnic individuals and communities. Some of the best ways to improve our understanding of others is by being curious, suspending preconceptions, asking questions, and listening.

As roles for teachers expand, teacher leadership will demand such competence. After all, to think critically, to become world citizens, and to imagine others' lives are essential actions in a democratic culture. In developing these competencies, this book can help.

Introduction
Finding Purpose

Given that the world is fractured by divisiveness, listening to dead voices might be our best hope for social justice.

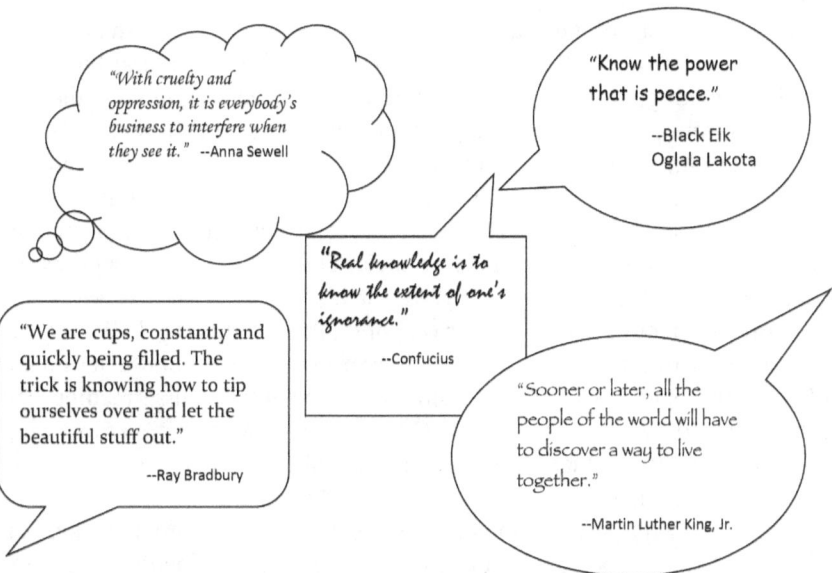

Although the speakers are dead, their words live on as inspiration to achieve a more nearly perfect world. They invite us to wonder what role we might play in contributing to humanity's peaceful coexistence.

Individuals in contemporary societies can amplify these disembodied voices and begin to live out the vision in their words by looking beyond the self, and one way of knowing and believing to accept alternatives. When we withhold judgment and are curious about unfamiliarity and difference, we adopt the eyes of an explorer. These eye-opening experiences may inspire us to speak out about diversity issues and to interrupt the fear that results in discriminatory attitudes and actions. With these "cultural lenses" (Delpit, 1995), we see more deeply and completely.

Preparing educators to develop cultural lenses is a prerequisite for culturally responsive teaching. These cultural lenses call on educators to embrace alternate perspectives and to be open to new ways of knowing. This ability to see comes largely from listening. Yet, speaking and listening are often marginalized in classrooms under the assumption that students can already hear and talk.

Hearing, however, is primarily a passive exercise, while listening commands active participation and focus. Listening calls on us to be emotionally present and to extend some measure of understanding so that we can see from another's vantage point or imagine an alternate experience. It requires that we hold two viewpoints to the light for closer examination and scrutiny. This kind of seeing and listening emerges during the cultivation of what often gets called multicultural literacy.

In 2007, an issue of the National Council of Teachers of English document, *Adolescent Literacy Policy Research Brief,* defined multicultural literacy as "seeing, thinking, reading, writing, listening, and discussing in ways that critically confront and bridge social, cultural, and personal differences. It goes beyond a 'tourist' view of cultures and encourages engagement with cultural issues" (Adolescent, 2007, p. 5). That a person identifies as Chinese is only one layer of self—besides its roots in race and ethnicity, cultural markers derive from socioeconomic status or social class, language, exceptionality, age, religion, gender identity, and geography.

Those nine factors determine our way of thinking, behaving, believing, and interacting with the world. To remind me of the nine common determinants of cultural identity as I selected literature for potential course reading lists, I used the acronym CLEAR GREG (Miller, 2014). With that memory aid, I could effortlessly produce the list: socioeconomic class, language, exceptionality, age, religion, gender, race, ethnicity, and geography.

As I continued to work with young adults, I noticed how much name, family, reputation, and perception of belonging contribute to identity formation. To accommodate this new insight, CLEAR GREG became GREEN APPLE (See figure 1.1).

Although the revised acronym doesn't include a separate letter for *race*, I consider race, which I relate to biological heritage, as distinct from ethnicity, which I define as referring to ancestry and to the customs or social practices that mark group membership, but all of the identifiers are interrelated and difficult to separate.

Gender Identity

Religion

Ethnicity and Race

Economic Class/Socioeconomic Status

Name/Family

Age

Place (geography, national territory)

Perception of Belonging

Language

Exceptionality — whether gifted or challenged

GREEN APPLE Acronym

People largely function in complex societies through learned behaviors. The ways in which we speak, our mannerisms, and our behaviors all signal who we are and establish norms for social interaction. Our attitudes, preferences, needs, and behaviors differ with changes in context and circumstances—making any real understanding difficult.

Although I was using GREEN APPLE as a guide for understanding my students and for selecting literature and then pairing it with readers, I found myself inviting readers during literary discussions to focus on the distinct identifiers and to ask questions, to interrogate character behavior from that angle—in other words, to ask GREEN APPLE questions. Readers will learn more about the GREEN APPLE acronym and GREEN APPLE questions in subsequent chapters of this book.

While I don't consider the questions to be the same as a literary theory or a critical approach to teaching adolescent literature as described by Appleman (2009) or Latrobe and Drury (2009), the GREEN APPLE questions do work similarly. Like critical lenses, the questions provide readers with another kind of analytical tool that helps them to "see" differently, illuminating an identity element for closer scrutiny.

When we read a text with this kind of "lighting," we suddenly see what before was invisible. The questions not only illuminate different perspectives on a character's behavior, for example, but make readers aware that their experiences also color a reading of a text.

The more research I did, the more confusing and layered I realized the topic of culture can be, so this book attempts to share ONE way of approaching the complex topics of culture and identity. Many alternate interpretations certainly exist, but classroom teachers are in a unique position to bring this multifaceted topic to young people at a time of learning readiness and at a time when society gravely needs interventions that promote social justice.

Although the GREEN APPLE approach may at first seem oversimplified, that is not my intention. My intention is to make a convoluted topic more manageable and more accessible so that we talk about cultural differences more frequently and recognize that the influence of these traits is not fixed or permanent. Culture is a fluid, negotiable, and dynamic quality. Gay (2000) agrees, calling culture "a dynamic system of social values, cognitive codes, behavioral standards, worldviews, and beliefs used to give order and meaning to our own lives as well as the lives of others. . . . Culture determines how we think, believe, and behave . . . and how we teach and learn" (pp. 8–9).

Through the reading, writing, speaking, listening, creative, and critical thinking activities in *Honoring Identities*, teachers can guide this discovery process. As global connectedness becomes more and more a common reality, the need for cultural tolerance and global understanding is becoming increasingly important. Time invested in this book's literacy activities contributes to a life of knowledge sharing and empathy building. Teachers who value these contributions to a meaningful life will make time for cultivating them.

Honoring Identities argues that creating culturally responsive learning communities is a process which begins with respecting students' home cultures (chapter 1), building community and connections (chapter 2), cultivating certain student and teacher dispositions (chapter 3), nurturing social justice (chapter 4), leveraging the power of talk and dialogic exchange (chapter 5), using Cultural Identity Literature (CIL) to build bridges and to normalize difference (chapter 6), and fostering a culture of civil discourse (chapter 7).

The book is organized in this fashion to reflect how learning originates with the individual and depends on relationship building and forming connections—both with information and with other humans. These branches lengthen with cultivation and nurturing and with the cross-pollination that accompanies idea sharing—encountering new perspectives and swelling with possibility. All of this incoming data requires that we organize, analyze, evaluate, and grow our thinking. Some of these ideas we will savor; others we will discard as we define and redefine who we are and how our lives will play out. Being culturally conscious and respectful of others prepares us to face the world and still remain culturally connected.

Introduction 5

This book and its topics come at a time when authors are responding to the call for more diverse books and as teachers and librarians work to diversify their shelves. Selecting books with the GREEN APPLE cultural markers in mind will ensure that an array of identities receives inclusion and develops a sense of belonging.

Cultural Identity Literature and dialogic exchange guided by the GREEN APPLE acronym aren't panaceas, but as learning tools they encourage cultural border crossing, seeing from multiple perspectives, challenging dominant modes of knowing, and producing knowledge from facts. With such bridge building, we can mitigate human cruelty and the tendency to hate, reject, or ignore what one doesn't know or even try to understand.

With the help of *Honoring Identities,* teachers can construct and put into practice a variety of approaches to the texts they and their future students will read. Whether teachers use the GREEN APPLE questions, a Pause and Ponder moment, or one of the other critical thinking strategies presented in this book to facilitate cross-cultural comprehension, they are training themselves and their students to read beneath layers built by preference and familiarity.

Chapter One

Cultural Identity

Every decision we make is informed by who we are and where we come from. Our roots not only keep us grounded, they serve as transport systems. The communities in which we are nurtured determine how we grow, how we interpret the world, and what psychological schema and scripts we develop. Like plants imbibing nutrients, we absorb ideas that affect our thinking. Just as roots anchor a plant, place, family, heritage, and community all provide a foundation for our very being. We all benefit if we take the time to learn about one another.

Abenaki author Joseph Bruchac shares evidence of these truths in his book *Hidden Roots* (2004), a story that discusses the key role that ancestral heritage plays in shaping our identities and how life doesn't work well lived in hiding. Readers of this young adult novel will learn the value in respecting the heritage and history of all people.

Despite our experiences' ability to influence us, however, they don't necessarily define us in the strictest sense of the word, which means *to describe exactly* or *to mark out or fix limitations*. Humans are not so easily pinned down and classified; we don't make good statistical machinery. Furthermore, humans are adaptable, resilient, and able to survive uprooting and transplanting. So, even though our origins, our roots, play a crucial role in shaping us, we grow into individuals as a result of our personal choices and how we react to our experiences.

Because we are the authors of our own life stories, and the power to revise that story is often within our control, the question of *Who Am I* is going to have different answers at different times in our lives; these evolutions make life interesting. Sometimes we trap ourselves with our own doubts. We may perceive that men have power over women, that limited means are commensurate with power so that the wealthy have more choices, or that we have no choice.

While those perceptions may hold truths and the family and circumstances into which we are born certainly impose limitations over which we often have little control, we also need to fully explore our options and tap our resources, reaching out to others and asking for their help or working ourselves to effect change.

Given these definitions and realities, we might do well to shift our focus in communication arts from language conventions to social practices. Without such investigation to regard students' home cultures, educators may draw unwarranted conclusions that negatively impact the learning environment.

A home culture, one's identity, is determined by eleven common factors: gender identification; religion; ethnicity and race; economic class/socioeconomic status; name/family; age; place (geography/national territory); language (discourse community); and exceptionality—whether gifted or challenged (GREEN APPLE). These factors determine a person's way of thinking, feeling, believing, and behaving. Culturally responsive teaching addresses all eleven determinants.

As Anaïs Nin (1961), a French-American essayist and novelist, insightfully observed, "We don't see things as they are; we see them as we are" (p. 124). Based on past experiences, we think something should look a certain way, so we "see" it that way. Published author and educational researcher Lisa Delpit (1995) also noted:

> We do not really see through our eyes or hear through our ears, but through our beliefs. To put our beliefs on hold is to cease to exist as ourselves for a moment. . . . It means turning yourself inside out, giving up your own sense of who you are, and being willing to see yourself in the unflattering light of another's angry gaze. It is not easy, but it is the only way to learn what it might feel like to be someone else and the only way to start the dialogue. (pp. 46–47)

Nin and Delpit both observe how experience clouds our vision of reality, that what we see is filtered through cognitive bias. Every truth is refracted and discolored by the light of personal perception.

Sir Francis Bacon called these *idols*—false images that defy scientific reasoning (Hall, 2013). These obstructions include the human tendency to follow preconceived ideas about things, to harbor preferences, and to accept social conventions or the media as truth. Such tendencies lead to the type of blindness that Nin and Delpit describe. Although our impressions are real to us, we must remember that not everyone shares our reality; other realities exist. Delpit proposes that classroom teachers lead the way in adjusting our vision by offering diverse groups the opportunity to learn about each other.

Such learning will involve confronting issues of power and privilege that dominate current social practices, asking questions about our world, seeing beyond stereotypes, and welcoming alternate ways of knowing and being. Preconceived notions about such subjects as gender, ability, and beauty affect not only how we react to others but also how we see them.

With a cultural lens, we aspire to sharpen or alter our vision, so that a photograph of a trailer home, a wrecked car in the backyard, and laundry hung on a line doesn't shout poverty and deprivation but can speak of the pride a parent has after having saved enough money to move out of a yardless apartment into a trailer where an abandoned car provides a place for all the neighborhood children to gather and play out imaginative adventures.

Through education and empathy building, we can cross the border into cultural understanding. A deeper, more complex understanding of culture should better prepare potential educators to teach in a multiethnic, multilingual, economically-stratified society. Challenging our own biases and taking stock of our own values will provide opportunities to reflect on our own identity and possible privilege before we teach children from diverse backgrounds. An exercise for performing this reflection occurs in chapter 6.

WHAT IS CULTURE?

Although social scientists don't agree on any one definition of culture, some definitions are widely accepted. One of the older definitions of culture was provided in 1871 by British anthropologist Sir Edward Burnett Tylor: "Culture is that complex whole which includes knowledge, belief, art, morals, law, customs, and other capabilities and habits ACQUIRED by man as a member of society" (quoted in Banks, 2010, p. 35; emphasis added). Mead (2003) goes further to clarify the difference between *culture*, "the system of transmitted and LEARNED behavior of all human beings" (p. 16), and *a culture*, which defines the "particular forms of behavior that belong to a particular group of people . . . a society that has developed through history" (p. 16; emphasis added).

Although capitalization highlights the major difference in the two definitions, the term *acquiring* implies learning from the culture in which we are raised. Both suggest culture is a social construct and that we are not born with any innate culture.

Erickson (2010) calls culture a "primary human toolkit," claiming "culture consists of the patterning of the practices of 'doing being human'—in our routine actions, in our interpretations of meanings in those actions, and in the beliefs that underlie our meaning interpretations" (p. 35). Banks (2010) similarly suggests culture "consists of the shared beliefs, symbols, and interpretations within a human group. . . . People in a culture usually interpret the meanings of symbols, artifacts, and behaviors in the same or in similar ways" (p. 8).

In its most reduced state, then, culture refers not only to who I am but who we are, which implies an individual identity as well as group identities. We live out our beliefs, enacting dispositions that guide our actions. Acculturated to rules and norms for behavior, we live and act subconsciously, so conditioned by culture that we don't see it.

Using these definitions, one can see how culture emerges from groupings with shared values, beliefs, and ways of being in the world. Wrestlers, writers, cooks, and clerks all share similar group interests, understandings, and a language unique to their individual communities. Those outside the culture or group may struggle to communicate due to language barriers or value differences. Unless you're a wrestler, for example, you may not understand terminology like *pin, take-down,* or *near fall,* and you may not agree with dieting practices or the discipline of training regimens. Those within the community, however, prize their vernacular and their values and will vigorously defend them. Cultures can clash when we disregard the notion of cultural multiplicity, the role of interpretation in communication, and the impact of misinterpretation.

Among the skills vital to human survival are the abilities to imagine, to conceive of alternative ways of life, and to entertain new ideas. Multicultural literacy—with its focus on speaking and listening—highlights these essentials. Such training calls on us to embrace alternate perspectives, to be open to new ways of knowing, and to learn to look beyond ourselves. We're surrounded by culture, acculturated to rules and norms to the point that we don't even realize they're there.

Being curious, withholding judgment, and asking questions while keeping GREEN APPLE—with its eleven elements to explicitly consider—in mind brings on new forms of knowledge and sharpens our cultural lenses so that we are better able to perceive how others might experience the world. With this shared awareness, we are more inclined to empathize than to judge or to hate. We are more inclined to wonder, what would I do if this were happening to me? Questioning opens the door to communication and potentially brings on new forms of knowledge.

As students grapple with identity, all eleven of the GREEN APPLE elements are influential factors. To deny any of these factors or to exclude them, in effect, erases the unique experiences which shape who we are. In order to become self-aware of our cultural significance, we all need to develop cultural awareness.

WHAT SCHOOLS CAN DO

School is also a culture, one that sometimes works against rather than in tandem with the home culture. For members of the nondominant group, the gulf between home and school can be confusing or even devastating. Educators have a responsibility to work as liaisons between the two cultures, to act as cultural brokers between their students and the school or academic culture, to serve as "sponsors of literacy," to use Deborah Brandt's (2001) term.

Research shows that new knowledge is more accessible and retained longer when it is connected to prior knowledge and to familiar references. Connecting home literacy practices to school-based literacies is crucial. In this bridge building, to create effective learning settings, the components of culture that matter most include systems of language, reflection of core values, and adoption of culturally responsive behaviors that shape the context and the content of the classroom.

For instance, even a seemingly insignificant detail as hyphenating African American can send a message. Some ethnic groups consider the hyphen a symbol of marginalization. Similarly, a dominant society member or an exclusive group will often get a noun referent while subordinates get adjectives. Political activist Gloria Steinem (2007) points this out: "Just as there are 'novelists' and then 'women novelists,' there are 'movies' and then 'chick flicks.' Whoever is in power takes over the noun—and the norm—while the less powerful get an adjective" (p. 303).

Other observations about language can reveal cultural values. Notice how the word *I* begins many sentences in the English language: "I dropped the bottle." This is an example of how language can carry the cultural notion of rugged individualism. But, other cultures may conceptualize the world differently. For example, in Spanish, one might say "*Dejé la botella,*" which roughly translates to "the bottle dropped or fell from me." This version reflects rugged pluralism, suggesting that humans are not alone; we are partners to the things of this world. Thus, passive language is a construct of worldview.

While social welfare and justice are goals for most social agencies, schools can do much to shape this reality, a reality that may reside in a greater attention to developing multicultural literacy. While the human brain is hardwired for joy, anger, surprise, disgust, sadness, and fear, all other emotions must be taught (Jensen, 2009). Many of these are prized by, even essential to, functional social systems: humility, forgiveness, empathy, optimism, compassion, patience, cooperation, and gratitude. Without such teaching, divisiveness arises.

Until we teach social and emotional skills, we can expect students to be disrespectful, to blurt inappropriate language, to behave impulsively, and to see only themselves. With cultural lenses, we develop a culturally responsive mindset, a mindset that embraces alternate perspectives. Culturally responsive schooling (CRS) recognizes, respects, and uses students' identities and backgrounds as meaningful sources for creating optimal learning environments.

The goal of CRS is to produce students who see beyond themselves and who possess knowledge and competencies in both mainstream and home societies. In reaching this goal, educators can focus on the formula ABC^4—affirming identity, building community, and cultivating curious, creative, and critical thinking.

Building culturally responsive mindsets starts with affirming identity through community building and continues with developing certain dispositions, nurturing social justice, using dialogue pedagogy, and building bridges with Cultural Identity Literature (CIL) selected to represent the key facets of identity and then approached with GREEN APPLE questioning. This book proposes to help with the important mission of building culturally responsive mindsets. But building is a process, one that will require patience.

One of the most challenging considerations of CRS and the GREEN APPLE approach will be managing doubt, because as CIL promotes other ways of seeing, revision may mean letting go of long-held beliefs. How we respond to others and how we live our own lives are subject to change when we read and discuss with added insight. Cultural Identity Literature supported by dialogic exchange and technology can transport us to places where we can discover, experience, and be transformed in the process.

As Mark Twain once said, "Travel is fatal to prejudice, bigotry, and narrow-mindedness." When we have neither the time nor the monetary resources to travel and to collect cultural experiences first-hand, books and virtual reality provide surrogates. This truth implies that classrooms and libraries should diversify their shelves with a broad selection of books.

Books, especially CIL titles, enable us to hear stories of diverse people living in different places and accumulating alternate experiences. These stories help readers not only to realize that others have a story of their own but to encourage us to develop familiarity with what we might otherwise perceive of as strange. Through the process of building culturally responsive mindsets, we train ourselves to be emotionally present and to extend some measure of understanding so that we can see from another's vantage point or imagine an alternate experience. And hopefully we can look beyond ourselves to embrace alternate or enlarged definitions of terms like *normal* or *minority*.

GREEN APPLE questions provide a training ground for civil discourse because they enable students to hear diversity of thought and to recognize that their reality, their understanding, their experience is not the only one. They learn to interrogate their biases, to consider alternatives, and to make room for new learning as they struggle against long-held assumptions, often planted by misinformed media messages or by provincial experiences.

This interrogation process will mean that more talk will happen in schools, not teacher talk but student talk. With texts carefully selected to inspire questions and to engage readers in interactive dialogue, thinking expands because talking is a road to understanding. In fact, contentious topics and the bold books that present them serve as a method for teaching civil discourse and making a difference in the world. Reading texts that feature tough topics not only imparts information but also assists readers in forming opinions after encountering multiple perspectives. Chapter 4 will address more fully the role bold books might play in promoting social justice.

Discussions stimulated by influential texts have the power to shift perspectives and to inspire lasting change. Learning about others has the potential to make our eyes different; we begin to look beyond the self and one way of knowing and believing, to accept alternatives. Opening the dialogue to meaningful discussion on diversity issues serves not only to enlighten and to build knowledge but to interrupt the hate that results in oppression, racism, and other discriminatory attitudes and actions. Silence is not an effective strategy; it is actually hindering our ability to develop comfort in interacting with those who are different from us—we need to talk about diversity issues so that we can cross lines of difference.

Schools can also strengthen their arts programs. Art has long been a recorder of history. To learn about a time period or to catch a glimpse of a people's values and beliefs, scholars need simply look to the art from that period. Music, theater, painting, prose, and poetry capture a slice of life, often serving it up raw. Art reveals a place of thinking, sometimes dreaming. It crosses boundaries and borders; it bears witness to personal, social, political, and economic identities. Chapter 2 will discuss art's role at greater length.

To embrace the truth in these ideas, consider music's power to influence the human condition or how photographs provide an ethnographic case study. Artists, a term meant to include authors here, collect data and make inferences about the world; they keep memory alive; their interpretations connect us to other cultures, offer a relationship with the world beyond the local, and lead us to places of respect for one another.

The arts not only have power to influence the human condition but also to help us understand the world in which we live. As a repository for artifacts, art further acts as a type of cultural encyclopedia—a reference, a decoder or translator of who we are as a people. As we individually escape into artistic creation, we discover potential; art renews our hopes and gives us reason to dream. Art provides a place to battle the demons in our lives and to survive the fight.

Chapter Two

Building Community and Connections

With the start of every school year, in an effort to acquaint themselves with their students and to develop community, teachers do well building into that first month a series of "getting to know you" writing activities. These invitations to write serve multiple additional purposes, allowing teachers to formatively assess the students they will be teaching and to provide them with important intel.

Meeting students where they are, knowing something about their writing aptitudes and other literacies, while also learning something about who they are enables teachers throughout the year to address students' needs, to honor their identities, and to pair them with reading materials that match their interests or meet their learning needs.

On day one, amidst the acclimation events, classes might engage in listing "ten things to know about me." The teacher might wish to disclose a model for the task, which can also serve as a means of self-introduction. After that sharing, the teacher can invite students to share information they'd like the teacher to know. From these lists, teachers can learn passions, hobbies, anxieties, and other useful details that might aid them in planning curriculum. Later, these same lists can be recycled in the English/Language Arts classroom as a syntax mini-lesson to instruct writers about using variety in sentence beginnings to enhance fluency and rhythm.

With a formative assessment of Kylee's list in textbox 2.1, a teacher might detect that Kylee varies sentence beginnings and uses detail effectively. A teacher will likely also notice three uses of the word *love*, revealing that this writer might benefit from a craft mini-lesson to address word choice variety. In another mini-lesson, the teacher may discuss the cognitive challenge presented by passive voice and the circumstances under which a writer might wish to use that construction. Based on the interests the writer has revealed, the teacher might recommend books that feature female athletes, nature, family, or dogs. The writer also alludes to some promising topics for future writing.

> **TEXTBOX 2.1: TEN THINGS TO KNOW ABOUT KYLEE**
>
> I love to play sports and games, which bring out the fierce competitor in me.
> As a result of adoring the warmth of the outdoors, I love going barefoot while the grass tickles my feet.
> Bright purple, yellow, green, and blue match my bright and exciting uniqueness.
> Laughing and joking around lets me have a good time and creates a more lively, exciting situation.
> Pushed by the motivation of my family, I strive to work my hardest in school and sports.
> I love sleeping in when I get to, which is about *9:30* at the latest.
> And, it is a nuisance to me whenever people act disrespectfully or wear mismatched socks.
> Many exciting memories with my role model and sister are made as we share laughter, whether through work or play.
> Every once in a while, I love to go camping and take pleasure in the outdoors.
> Working with my dog, Sassy, I feel a sense of accomplishment when I teach her new tricks and lessons.

These lists, when shared in a Sharing Circle, build community as students get to know one another. A Sharing Circle is a discussion strategy in which students sit in a circular formation. Research has shown that these arrangements encourage an attitude of cooperation, support, and team building. Because everyone can see and hear one another, the circular set-up facilitates communication, encourages more participation, and boosts collaboration.

Because a circular seating arrangement isn't hierarchical, people are more likely to feel that they're valued. They're also more likely to share their ideas. This arrangement generally communicates the message that all members are expected to contribute and that their opinions have collateral—that they count. It also promotes a collective mindset.

During such sharing, students will hopefully notice that communities all feature differences, differences that add to the uniqueness and beauty of a group. Teachers typically wish for their students to know that when we are all different, we can learn from one another, and with the insight gained we can respect each other. After all, difference is not dangerous, nor is it a defect or a burden.

BUILDING COMMUNITY THROUGH WRITING

Other writing activities that provide essential information about students and also develop community include Bio-Poems, I Am Poems, and imitations of the poem "Raised by Women" by Kelly Norman Ellis (2003). These writing strategies are often used in National Writing Project work.

Another powerful invitation derives from writing narrative poems prompted by the three children's books *Momma, Where Are You From?* by Marie Bradby (2000), *If You're Not from the Prairie* . . . by David Bouchard (1995), and *When I Was Young in the Mountains* by Cynthia Rylant (1982).

Lists patterned after the one Arnold Spirit writes in Sherman Alexie's novel *The Absolutely True Diary of a Part-Time Indian* (2007) provide insight into a person as well. After reading all of the tribes to which Arnold belongs, students might develop their own tribal affiliations or bands of belonging lists.

Models for many of these and directions to guide their construction can be found in the resources section following this chapter.

After weeks of writing, students collect and revise these various activities to hone writing abilities, to assemble multi-genre memoirs, and to better understand themselves and their classmates. In his book *Zigzag: A Life of Reading and Writing, Teaching and Learning,* (2008), Tom Romano defines multi-genre:

> A multi-genre paper arises from research, experience, and imagination. It is not an uninterrupted, expository monologue, nor a seamless narrative, nor a collection of poems. A multi-genre paper is composed of many genres and subgenres. Each piece works by itself, is self-contained, makes a point of its own. Yet all the pieces are connected by theme or topic and sometimes by language, images, and content. In addition to many genres, a multi-genre paper often contains many voices, not just the author's. The craft demanded of the writer is to make such a paper hang together as one. (p. 184)

To write a multi-genre memoir, students frame their memoirs with an introduction and a conclusion. In between, they use pieces that illustrate who they are and how they came to be that person. Teachers might further instruct students to select from the various pieces they have written, choosing to incorporate parts or whole scripts. They can encourage the use of photographs or artifacts that capture cultural events, traditions, ceremonies, and celebrations shared by the family.

Some of the elements these writers wish to use in creating their multi-genre memoirs may not be authored by them, and this is okay. Maybe there is a guiding quote or some words of wisdom or a story passed down and shared by an elder or from an author who has always provided inspiration. Perhaps a song saved them from despair or aligns with their life philosophy. Students should be encouraged to include elements like these as well.

Once students have gathered myriad elements, these can be arranged to tell their stories. Students will create transitions from piece to piece and write the fill-in details to flesh out the narrative while providing the essential links for maintaining fluency. Thinking in jigsaw puzzle or collage mode, they move the pieces around to capture the greatest artistic and compositional effect, organizing pieces of writing so that those with parallel or similar themes or thought threads follow one another.

With transitional links, draft lead-ins, and colons, writers can achieve a fluid and cohesive piece that illustrates, elaborates upon, and substantiates who they are as cultural beings and that defines the influences that have shaped or raised them. Framing the entire display with a fairly traditional introduction and conclusion ensures that the reader follows the thematic thread and that the memoir provides a cohesive definition.

Many of these models can also work effectively in teacher-training programs and in literature courses, where the formats might serve as reader response protocols, with students writing Bio-Poems or I Am Poems as character analyses or character sketches, for example. Discovering where students come from and embracing the notion of place as a component of culture, as a shaper of self and of identity, are critical to creating a culturally responsive classroom.

SHARED EXPECTATIONS

Community building also involves developing a set of shared expectations. Many teachers wish they could teach their students how to be students before the first day of class, and we might be able to do this with an exercise that invites a community of learners to consider the characteristics that make a good student and classmate.

After hearing/reading a book like Miriam Cohen's *First Grade Takes a Test* (2006) or *Have You Filled a Bucket Today?* by Carol McCloud (2007), students will be primed to think about the expectations we have for one another and for behavior and can develop a list of the qualities we look for in ourselves and in others. Instead of focusing on the top ten things to avoid, this listing activity focuses on the positive, and in a respectful tone, encourages students to take on these qualities.

As an introduction to a college Assessment in Education course, an instructor might write a reflection, like that illustrated below, to share with preservice teachers. Such a method invites teacher candidates not only to focus on the characteristics and dispositions often valued by teachers but to reveal expectations. In the process, they experience an activity they may wish to implement in their own classrooms someday. Doing a survey like this on the first day of any class serves to begin the relationship-building process while also enabling instructors to discover what the students in their classrooms value:

1. On the first day of class, I look for a positive attitude, a willingness to try new things, and a growth mindset. I like the fresh way young people look at learning with wonder in their eyes. I value their confidence, their courage, and their optimism. Focused on opportunity, students are often anticipating the new semester and how much they will learn.
2. Students with minds open to knowledge are receptive to learning. They may have come to my class to fulfill a requirement but decide to make the most of the experience, taking ownership of their learning and personalizing it with their own creative twist to the various learning experiences. Their final products exhibit time investment, innovation, and critical thinking.
3. Students with hearts open to compassion also care about the learning of their classmates. They see learning as a cooperative enterprise and willingly, patiently assist their classmates. These students know that error and failures are part of the learning process.
4. The first day of class is made even better by students who arrive early, ready to make the course their own and to accept responsibility for their learning. After all, learning is not a passive act; it requires the consent and activity of the learner. These students establish goals and standards for their performance because they know that success depends on preparation for and investment in class activities, as well as on timely completion of learning experiences.
5. Intelligence is not innate; it is developed through effort, motivation, and persistence in the face of struggle. Productive persistence—struggling through difficulty—requires a student to fight past the pain, to trust that meaning will come with perseverance. A lightbulb will only glow when the learner completes the circuit with energy. Instead of feeling intimidated, such students are inspired by a challenge.

6. I appreciate students who share eye contact during a lecture. Standing in front of a group of students and presenting ideas is hard work, so seeing eyes engaging with me rather than with a device screen makes this difficult job so much easier. Thank you to those who listen, nod, ask questions, participate in conversation, and otherwise engage with your professors.
7. Students who come to me when they need help prove they are willing to invest the time and effort that learning requires. The learner has identified an obstacle and is addressing it by seeking assistance. Teaching is a passion of mine because helping someone learn a difficult concept is incredibly rewarding. I am relieved when students recognize that they need help and come to me early enough to get it.
8. My students, I anticipate our time together with pleasure. I enjoy visiting with you, mentoring you, teaching you, learning from you, and watching you interact and learn from one another. Your achievement brings me satisfaction.

With agreed-upon standards for behavior, educators not only have student investment and ownership, they have a unified vision and a shared vocabulary that they can use to call students to task as they make a commitment to be firm, be fair, and be kind.

This commitment to kindness should also extend to the self. Just as students need to be taught protocols for responding politely and constructively to one another so that trust can build among members of the class, they will need to be kind to themselves, giving themselves permission to make mistakes. This topic is discussed at greater length in chapter 3, but when students see failure as part of the learning process and not as a reflection on themselves, they are more likely to persist in an area of struggle. After all, struggle is nothing to be ashamed of; it means learning is happening.

To build community, study geography, and share cultural knowledge, a valuable book is *My House Has Stars* (Orchard Books, 1996) by Megan McDonald. The book's sixteen pages feature eight richly descriptive vignettes. Readers or listeners will visit geographically and culturally diverse homes from Nepal, the Philippines, a village in Ghana, the islands of Japan, an adobe pueblo, a yurt in the Mongolian desert, a Brazilian city skyscraper, and an igloo in Alaska that all share the same roof: a star-soaked sky.

This children's book has been used effectively with audiences from elementary to college levels as a writing prompt to describing home, which might be one's headquarters, one's backdrop, one's framework, one's history, and one's haven. The book might also serve to stimulate geography lessons for upper elementary students, and it effectively opens the humanities conversation for all audiences.

After all, the individual, the I, is the agent responsible for finding the ties that bind humankind. Readers likely will have noticed that the term *humanities* contains the words *human* and *ties* connected by an *I*. Subliminally, the term acts as a messenger, speaking of the humanities' power to humanize us, sharing the hope that human action can solve social problems, can help us bridge differences, and can knit the rents in the social fabric. This action starts with the individual.

At their core, literature, the ancient rhetorics, poetry, and all other forms of art endeavor to tie us in collaborative harmony. Books like McDonald's celebrate the multiplicity of several cultures, each with its unique stories, geographical features, creatures, smells, foods, vocabularies, and cultural beliefs and practices. But despite their differences, these multiple cultures share commonalities.

While some might suggest that the world is fractured by divisiveness and that a perfect world is not possible, education and educators can contribute to a more nearly perfect world by building bridges to social justice. This bridge building begins in community building and by forming connections. Study of the humanities provides a means for this learning to transpire.

FAVORING THE HUMANITIES

In 2010, while speaking to the Arizona Humanities Council in Tempe, Arizona, poet Naomi Shihab Nye asked: "Is empathy the key note to social sustainability?" She went on to posit that art can lead us to places of respect for one another, a fact she demonstrates in her poem "Gate A-4" (2008). Besides illustrating the power of human compassion and connection, the poem confirms that hearing one another's stories is a form of cultural diplomacy (Miller, 2012).

The poem further defines communication as an essential ingredient in the transfer of emotion and reveals the power of language to inextricably link and to heal us: "The minute she heard any words she knew—however poorly used—she stopped crying" (Nye, 2008, p. 162). Hope for unity, for communication across cultural lines—what Nye describes in her poem as "the shared world"—is not lost if we take the time to listen, to connect, to share. We redefine and remake ourselves; we become different people as we read more, talk more, and write more. When we hear people's stories and when we accept new ways of knowing, we can reduce ignorance, grow hope, and diminish hate.

Philosopher and author Martha Nussbaum (2010) similarly posits that the fate of a democratic future hinges on the humanistic disciplines. She argues that American education is in crisis. Rather than developing "complete citizens who can think for themselves, criticize tradition, and understand the significance of another person's suffering and achievements" (p. 2), education is producing "useful machines" focused on profit and economic gain. Nussbaum calls this crisis a cancer capable of damaging the future of democratic self-government. For her, humanities and the arts are not "useless frills." From the humanities, we learn to think carefully, to challenge our assumptions, and to break out of received assumptions.

While the humanities (and arts) are certainly not the only conduit to these essential democratic faculties, they are one powerful avenue for nurturing those habits. These abilities to think critically, become a world citizen, and imagine others' lives sympathetically are crucial in a democratic culture; the alternative—conformity—speaks of puppetry and totalitarian regimes.

Social scientist Howard Gardner (2008), renowned for both his Multiple Intelligences and his Five Minds Theories, also desires greater focus on the humanities. As a citizen of the twenty-first century, living in a world that honors the STEM disciplines (science, technology, engineering, and mathematics), he wants to see more than the disciplined mind developed.

Gardner outlines his concern in his book *Five Minds for the Future* (2008) and worries particularly about the humanities: "I believe that one cannot be a full person, let alone have a deep understanding of our world, unless one is rooted as well in art, literature, and philosophy" (p. xviii).

As young minds are prepared for the future, Gardner aspires to see literature, music, philosophy, and history presented in ways that speak to a new generation and that address issues of current concern. Teachers can contribute to the difficult work of this teaching, to the fostering of humanitarian habits of mind, and to an awareness of the power of art with young adult literature (YAL), especially Cultural Identity Literature (CIL).

Young adult authors like those featured in resource 2.6 address the healing power of art while also commenting on art as a vehicle for discovering identity. All of these authors seem to suggest that art carries not only an element of catharsis and discovery but also a transformative power. Although art helps us understand the world in which we live, somehow, it also connects us to our humanity and to the nuances of relationships. Zitlow and Stover (2011) argue for "using art to order [life's] chaos" (p. 34). They describe how YAL provides a bridge to self-discovery and how art can help teens "better negotiate the difficult waters of adolescence" (p. 35).

Implementing books with explicit humanitarian and CIL themes potentially encourages critical and independent thinking while supporting youth agency, inviting engagement, and sponsoring literacy.

CATCHING FIRE REVEALS THE POWER OF ART

One book with a strong art-as-healing motif, *Catching Fire* (2009) by Suzanne Collins, captured the interest of adolescent readers in 2010, when it sat as number one on YALSA's Teens' Top Ten list. Collins' dystopian novel is the second in a trilogy about Katniss Everdeen and Peeta Mellark after their experience in the Hunger Games arena, the Capitol's sadistic and tyrannical means to inspire fear and maintain control.

This installment in the saga reveals the two teens seeking retaliation against President Snow, a predatory leader who doesn't just have blood on his hands but blood on his breath. A satyric man, he is fond of unrestrained revelry, lecherous in his use and abuse of power and in his disregard for human life.

Realizing they are pawns in a political game, Katniss and Peeta both decide to defy the Capitol and give hope to the rebels with their final messages to the Games' designers. As a means to send that message, they use art, transforming art into activism. Peeta paints Rue, capturing and memorializing her in those moments after her death in the Hunger Games arena. Because of Rue's senseless death, Katniss, who wished to send a message to the Capitol, had bedecked Rue with a floral shroud—a gesture of both defiance and love.

In her current act of rebellion, Katniss designs a soft sculpture and hangs an effigy of Seneca Crane (p. 237) to mimic how the Capitol put him to death for allowing two tributes to live in the Hunger Games. Although their thinking is called forbidden, Peeta wants to hold the government accountable, and Katniss considers her boldness proof that they might be able to kill her in body but not in spirit. She refuses to play the Games by the Capitol's rules; she's willing to be a martyr for the cause.

Besides using art to reclaim his power, Peeta utilizes his talent as a baker, painter, and illustrator in an attempt to showcase beauty in a world gone rotten. During the meeting with President Snow, Katniss' mother serves cookies that feature Peeta's frosting work: "They are beautifully iced with softly colored flowers" (p. 22). The cookie that Katniss crushes during her conference with President Snow displays a tiger lily, a flower revealing both art and symbolism.

According to the website Epic Gardening (Tiger Lily, 2019), in traditional lore, the tiger lily represents the fierceness and confidence of women. In addition, tiger lilies are a hardy, resilient, and aggressive flower—once cut from the stem, another blossom will quickly replace it, and if not pruned often, tiger lilies can quickly overtake an entire garden. These features all relate to Katniss, the girl on fire, proclaiming she is a force to be reckoned with.

Peeta also paints the Games—the detail is rich, the colors vivid, and the likeness so exact that Katniss responds, "I can almost smell the blood, the dirt, the unnatural breath of the mutt" (p. 53). In an effort to take the power from his haunting dreams, Peeta paints. Art is his method for tapping his courage, his way to "stop running and turn around and face whoever wants [him] dead" (p. 118). Art also distracts Peeta's mind, giving him something else to focus on: "I [Katniss] like to watch his hands as he works, making a blank page bloom with strokes of ink, adding touches of color to our previously black and yellowish book" (p. 161).

A third Collins character who knows the power of art is Cinna. Whether designing wedding dresses, costumes that glow like coal embers, or a dress that spins out to reveal a feathery mockingjay, Cinna channels his emotions into his work. He is a true artist with cloth and makeup and hair. In fact, his tremendous creativity and his use of art as activism gets him killed.

Ultimately, Collins suggests that art has power to influence the human condition; she presents characters who use art to escape oppression and to cope with adversity. As Zitlow and Stover (2011) report, "Introducing students to such characters is one option for providing them with productive ways of making sense of their pain and confusion" (p. 35). Collins' characters also encourage students to question the status quo and to think critically about social issues like oppression, tyranny, and socioeconomic disparity.

FOSTERING HUMANITIES-BASED AND HUMANITARIAN CONVERSATIONS

Although Jimi Hendrix proclaims "Music doesn't lie. If there is something to be changed in the world, then it can only happen through music," that transformational power is not unique to music, as readers glean from Collins' book.

Long ago, Plato outlined three castes in his *Republic*: Producers, Auxiliaries, and Guardians. As members of the Guardian caste, teachers nurture the intellectual, athletic, artistic, creative, and altruistic aspects of their students. The humanities enable and empower educators in that important humanitarian work, and a plethora of young adult books provide a map. As cultural voices, these authors as artists work for the betterment of the world.

As they read these words, adolescents also read their world. Young adult books like Collins' and like those in the annotated bibliography of resource 2.6, as well as the CIL titles listed in this book's appendix and those named in chapter 4 textbox 4.2, provide interesting and complex ideas to talk and argue about. They supply an ideal platform for youth to notice differences, think critically, consider alternate positions, and make more informed, ethical choices. Those in resource 2.6 also prescribe art as an antidote to pain and confusion.

When curricula foster conversations about books that focus on humanitarian and cultural identity concerns, they provide the opportunity to read, to write, and to argue about issues in a relevant context. Critical questioning exposes youth to situations that encourage a critical stance so as to inspire wisdom that might lead to an improved way of living in the world.

Wishing to steer away from controversy, teachers often hesitate to discuss contentious social issues or to conduct the conversations encouraged by critical theory pedagogy, but the process begins when teachers make stimulating materials available and allow the asking of questions. Of provocative texts, students will likely ask: "What is happening and how did it get this way?"

According to McNeil (1999), "the main goal of this curriculum is to help students see different kinds of knowledge, to understand how knowledge is constructed or how it reflects a given social context, and to make their own knowledge" (p. 165). The goal is not to seek homogeneous interpretations but to welcome diversity and encourage young people to negotiate their own meaning, to argue with the interpretations of others, and to make sense of popular culture in terms of their own values.

Educators will need to monitor this talk for the accountability levels referred to in chapter 5 and may need to remind students that the point of a discussion is not to win but to broaden their views and to learn something new.

Perhaps now more than ever, we need a pedagogy that integrates the critical thinking skills essential to raising social consciousness, to protocols that explore multiple views. With wars raging across the globe, with heightened concerns about terrorism, and with a global tendency toward polarization and a demonizing of those who hold differing opinions, learning these humanizing processes might have supreme relevance and currency. A growing body of YAL provides a core for that humanitarian learning.

Looking again at the word humanities, one notices that the *I* is nearly central. This positioning suggests the individual's potential role in the effort at creating human ties. As Mahatma Gandhi directed, "*I* must be the change I wish to see in the world." When horror haunts life—whether as terrorism or violence, as upset or upheaval—the question should be, *what can I do?* The authors of the books listed in resource 2.6 suggest we turn to art. Art slows us down, forcing us to notice and to cherish small details, details that disaster has the power to erase. In *19 Varieties of Gazelle* (2002), Nye claims: "We need poetry for nourishment and noticing, for the way language and imagery reach comfortably into experience, holding and connecting it more successfully than any news channel we could name" (p. xvi).

This focus on the humanities teaches us that art's job is not only to look nice; art has something to say. In this role as spokesman and sage, today's young adult books possess immense potential. These books speak to adolescents, using their language and meeting their emotional needs as they are developing personal philosophies. They also illustrate art's power in the struggle against the demons in our lives; art contributes to identity development, to perspective building, and to survival. As we expand the canon, we expand minds with the offered diversity in perspective.

RESOURCE 2.1: BUILDING A BIO-POEM

The Bio-Poem is a common format for presenting a character—either in literary response or in biography. Although the example below illustrates one version, numerous variations exist. Feel free to create a middle with more lines or different prompts than the sample shows. For example, you might wish to include additional lines about beliefs, desires, or dislikes. Also, if you wish to change words (i.e., *provides* instead of *gives*; *brother* instead of *relative*), you may take such liberties with this flexible format.

Line 1: first name
Line 2: a parallel series of four traits that describe (four adjectives) or rename (four nouns) your character; link these with the conjunction and
Line 3: relative of _____
Line 4: lover of _____, _____, and _____
Line 5: who feels _____, _____, and _____
Line 6: who needs _____, _____, and _____
Line 7: who fears _____, _____, and _____
Line 8: who gives _____, _____, and _____
Line 9: who would like to see _____, _____, and _____
Line 10: resident of _____ (this can be a geographic, intellectual, or imaginary place)
Line 11: last name

Expanding these lines with details, phrases, and clause extenders are keys to making this poem an interesting, fluent piece to read rather than a choppy and formulaic list. Be as accurate and complete in your description as possible.

The model below is a Bio-Poem written by a high school freshman for the character Shelly from *Flush* by Carl Hiaasen:

Shelly,

Daunting, stern, strong, and big-hearted
Girlfriend of Lice Peeking, the pathetic half drunk;
Lover of tangerine perfume, looking tough, and wearing multiple hoop earrings;
Who feels obligated to help Noah, scared about what has happened to Lice, and worthy—especially of more decent men;
Who needs money to help her survive, mostly after Lice took the last of hers; to give everyone a second chance, even her pathetic excuse for a boyfriend; and to help clear Paine Underwood's name;
Who fears almost no one, Dusty Muleman's getting away with polluting the ocean, and the safety of Noah and Abbey if they get caught on Operation Royal Flush;
Who provides the Coral Queen with a bartender, Noah with herself as an undercover spy, and some muscle to the trio of soon to be heroes (mostly Noah and Abbey, though);
Who would like to see Dusty behind bars, a new set of hoop earrings in her ears, and The Coral Queen shut down;
Resident of her rusty old trailer house in Florida,
Barbwire

RESOURCE 2.2: AUTHORS AND THEIR MENTOR TEXTS

Before reading/listening to any text, a teacher might invite students to use the "reading like a writer" strategy borrowed from Katie Wood Ray (1999) and to perform an inquiry analysis of the text. After listening for and noting craft moves, a class might talk about those techniques, naming them and discussing the impact they have on the text and why an author might choose to use techniques like parallel structure, personification, analogy, or absolute phrases, for example. Then, under the influence of the mentor text, students can write their own pieces, intentionally imitating the crafting techniques to achieve the action, fluency, tone, detail and imagery richness, or other desired effects.

The texts themselves prompt thinking, but to further generate thought with a text like *If You're Not from the Prairie . . .* by David Bouchard (1995), the teacher might draft and offer focus questions, like these:

- What is something about your experience that others might not be aware of?
- What is something that you know well about this topic but others might not?

- What smells, sounds, flavors, and other sensations can you add for descriptive detail?

From this exercise, and with inspiration from David Bouchard, a high school junior produced the following poem:

You Don't Know Me

If you're not from the farm, you don't know the farm,
you can't know all of the days spent tilling with the tractor,
sun beating on your neck, the growl of the tractor as it claws
and rips into the soil to create life for alfalfa.

If you're not from the farm, you can't know the farm.
You don't know how to shovel. You think you know how,
but you can't. The blade shapes the outcome of your crops
as it opens and closes the gateways for rushing irrigation water.

If you're not from the farm, you don't know the farm,
you can't know the joy. You think you know the joy,
but you don't. The excitement of seeing all of your hay in
and throwing a barn dance the next Saturday night
to celebrate with all of the other farmers,
eating pulled pork with corn on the cob and
juicy watermelon for dessert.

If you're not from the farm, you don't know the tractor,
you can't know the shovel, and you certainly don't know the joy.
If you don't know these things, you don't know me, how I act,
what I believe, or who I am. You can't know what I eat or
what I like; you can't see the soil in my veins, the plants in my skin,
or the wreckage of my hands, small tilling machines in themselves.
You may think you know me, but only the farm truly knows who I am.

RESOURCE 2.3: ELLIS MENTOR TEXT

For this next exercise, the teacher will need to secure a copy of the poem "Raised by Women" by Kelly Norman Ellis (2003). After reading the piece aloud, the teacher might lead students through the noticing and noting inquiry process. In this instance, the focus questions change:

- Who influenced you as you were growing up?
- What mannerisms and sayings make these people memorable?

- What chores, foods, traditions, pastimes, sayings, books, or movies/television shows have played a role in shaping who you are?

As writers notice the value of proper nouns and of sensory detail for adding specificity to their writing, they begin to use those crafting techniques, not only to personalize their writing but to add interest for the reader.

With inspiration from Kelly Norman Ellis, a high school freshman produced this piece:

Raised By

I was raised by
Action-packed
Page turning
Gary Paulsen writing
Kind of books.

I was raised by
Large, brown-eyed
Alfalfa munching
White flag waving
Type of deer.

I was raised by
Cheese smothered
Grease dripping
Fried onion covered
Mouth watering
County Fair quality
Sort of burgers.

I was raised by a
Fact finding
True story telling
History filled
Modern marveling
Kind of channel.

I was raised by a
Sugar-covered
Snapping
Crackling
Popping
Type of cereal.

I was raised by a
Sunset orange
Hair singeing
Smush-bun toasting
Smoky
Log devouring
Sort of fire.

I was raised by
These soul swaying
Character building
Kind of qualities

RESOURCE 2.4: BRADBY MENTOR TEXT

An inquiry of Marie Bradby's craft in *Momma, Where Are You From?* (2000) brings to mind routines, sounds and smells, foods, memorable people and snippets of conversation and interactions that link us to the past, concrete details of place, school memories, games played, chores performed, and music listened to. Focus Question: How has where you come from shaped who you've grown into?

After this prewriting and thinking, writers are usually ready to draft and then to revise.

Where I Come From

I am The One from Big Sky Country
miles of highways and dirt roads
and an eternity of wheat fields.

I am from swimsuits and caps,
goggles and earplugs,
coaches and teammates.

I am from blankets, clothes, and stuffed animals
enveloping me through a time capsule.
Pictures, letters, and mementos escape the capsule;
When I open the lid of the shoebox,
"How Much I Love You" and "Little Miss Muffet" are released.

I am from "Mom, they're hitting me" to "My brothers are better than your brothers." Inundated by G.I. Joes, Barbies, and Hot Wheel cars,
our day is filled at home.

I am from reading *Brown Bear Brown Bear*
and watching *Care Bears* to
playing Candy Land and learning embroidery at Grandma Darlene's.

I am from preparing lefsa and baking yams on Thanksgiving
and eating macaroni and cheese during swim meets.
I am from loving and understanding friends and family,
and it's where I'll always be from.
—High School Junior

*It might be of interest to know that The One was the personalized license plate on this young lady's car, not out of arrogance or cockiness but because her middle name is Theone and at swim meets she often heard, "You're the one from Montana," "You're the one who beat my time," or other versions of that phrase. She was encouraged by her family to be The One who wins.

RESOURCE 2.5: ALEXIE MENTOR TEXT

After hearing/reading Arnold Spirit's reflection about the tribes to which he belongs and the list that follows in the book's penultimate chapter, students can produce their own lists. After that prewriting, the teacher can invite them to flesh out those lists, to add detail to enrich and extend their membership in each of those "tribes."

The following Focus Questions can assist in the writing process:

- How do members of those tribes behave?
- What habits, mannerisms, and beliefs define them?
- What descriptive detail might you add that will allow someone else to be in that space/place with you?

By way of illustration, the teacher might then provide a model like that below:

Bands of Belonging

I belong to the tribe of Germans, large Catholic families, and rural country dwellers who live off the land and raise their own meat. I am a daughter, sister, mother, wife, friend, and teacher.

I find kinship with leaders and with people who love their work and wish "to be of use." I shoulder my burdens and plod forward, often without a map but certainly with a purpose, to grow hope and to leave an imprint with my high-expectations ethos.

I also worship at the shrine of Naïveté, the archaic deity who rewards worrying, adherence to traditions (like Saturday cookie and homemade bread baking and Sunday suppers), list-making, planning, and self-denial. However, this goddess and patron of hopeless romantics, those lovers of hugs and flowers and terms of endearment, invites an occasional glass or two of Merlot and condones indulgences of fresh raspberry-topped cheesecake.

Since I believe order and routine lend a sense of security and predictability to life's frenetic pace, I am an aficionado of routines. 5:30 a.m. finds me sitting in the semi-darkness, sipping Swiss chocolate almond coffee laced with cream while lulled by the relaxation of my glide rocker; exercise follows. I report to work by 7:30, watch Jeopardy at 6:00 in the evening, make my way to bed by 9:00, and correct papers or plan lessons in between. When I am troubled or angry, I clean to bring a feeling of control and order back to my life.

Besides my routines, I have ambitions and dreams, to never stop questioning or growing. After all, wisdom, deeply rooted in curiosity, gives birth to creativity. Thus, the tribe of voracious readers welcomes my membership, where I gladly pay my dues to escape into alternative worlds, to learn new perspectives, and to make connections.

These thoughts grow visible in my writing. I am a reviser, a word smith and grammar geek whose love for language hopefully infects the students I teach. Through writing we discover ourselves and learn to live our lives more intimately. Writing can provide emotional catharsis, seduce lovers, bond friendships, record memories, secure scholarships or jobs, win awards, ignite reform, motivate, inspire, and entertain.

Finally, I consort with the society of believers who revere gardens and walleye fishing holes as sacred nurturing places. While offering respite in fresh air cloaked with loon song or meadowlark warbling, these locations also provide a conquering grounds, a place to prove self-reliance and to reaffirm a sense of belonging.

RESOURCE 2.6: YA BOOKS FEATURING THE POWER OF ART

Alexie, S. (2007). *The Absolutely True Diary of a Parttime Indian*. New York: Little, Brown.

Using the humor motif and cartooning, Alexie demonstrates through his protagonist, Junior, how humor and poetry carry the power to save us from despair, from a loss of human identity, from genocide of the human spirit.

Anderson, L. H. (2001). *Speak*. New York: Penguin Putnam.

To heal from her silent depression, Melinda, a rape victim, draws trees. With the help of her art assignments, Melinda gains the perspective and strength to express her feelings. Ultimately, she reclaims her voice and speaks out against her attacker.

Carvell, M. (2002). *Who Will Tell My Brother?* New York: Hyperion.
To help him understand his cultural identity and how intricately it is tied to his past and to his ancestors, Evan draws hands.

Creech, S. (2004). *Heartbeat.* New York: HarperCollins.
In an effort to understand death, loss, and the power of perspective, Annie draws apples.

Fitch, J. (1999). *White Oleander.* New York: Little, Brown, and Company.
Astrid Magnussen and Paul Trout survive the cruelty life thrusts upon them, not the least of which are the travesties of the foster care system. If not for his cartoon artistry and graphic novel creation, readers question Paul's ability to survive just as readily as we observe the therapeutic power Astrid's art has for her. Whether painting, drawing, remaking her mother's letters sent from prison, or designing suitcases to capture the impact, influence, and personality of each of the mother figures in her life, Astrid discovers her identity, her humanity, and the transcendent power of art. True to the Old Norse origin of her name, Astrid finds beauty despite the ugliness and the unfairness of life.

Hyde, C. R. (2010). *Jumpstart the World.* New York: Alfred A. Knopf.
Elle has been abandoned by her mother whose wealthy new boyfriend Donald doesn't want to live with a teenager. So, at age fifteen, Elle has her own apartment and must learn to navigate the world without traditional support. The support she finds comes from unexpected friendships, especially from her neighbor Frank, who tells Elle: "That's why there's such a thing as activism. Sometimes you have to jumpstart the world just to get it to be what even the world admits it should be" (p. 143). With inspiration from Frank, Elle becomes an activist using a camera.

Koertge, R. (2003). *Shakespeare Bats Cleanup.* New York: Candlewick Press.
When fourteen-year-old Kevin Boland catches mononucleosis and is quarantined to his home, he discovers that keeping a journal and experimenting with poetry not only fills the monotonous hours but also helps him develop a stronger sense of self, make sense of his passions for baseball and girls, enrich his relationship with his father, and come to terms with his mother's death.

Paulsen, G. (1988). *The Island.* New York: Dell Publishing.

    Wil, like a contemporary Thoreau, discovers the wonders of nature through drawing herons, turtles, frogs, and fish, while also learning intimate details about his own identity.

Sandell, L. A. (2009). *A Map of the Known World.* New York: Scholastic.

    Cora and Damian both learn the redemptive power of art as they cope with the grief of Nate Bradley's death.

Chapter Three

Teacher and Student Dispositions

Written work performed during community building not only provides a teaching diagnostic but a glimpse into the lives of the students in the room. Knowing something about students' home cultures is a prerequisite for culturally responsive teaching. The writing invitations described in chapter 2 welcome the story of home and heritage into the classroom, a practice that honors the notion that all cultures contribute, that all voices deserve to be heard.

Effective instruction in any classroom requires that the teacher's instruction be informed not only by the content of the discipline but also by the lives of his or her students. When teachers take the time to know their students and to know the code of their primary discourse communities, they can build bridges for developing secondary discourses; teachers can sponsor literacy rather than create obstacles.

If popular progressive pedagogies like open classrooms, whole language, process writing, and writing workshops—while claiming to represent the best learning for all students—do not in fact match the learning needs of the culturally and linguistically diverse students with whom teachers work, they simply alter pedagogy so as not to silence some students while privileging others.

With such an approach, educators give all students access to the material presented. They recognize the full potential of each student and provide the challenges necessary for achieving that potential. When teachers communicate to students that they expect the students' best and that they shouldn't settle for less, students typically grow into those expectations.

All students will benefit if teachers invest the time planning learning experiences that enable students to learn about one another, if we work to build strong community partnerships, and if we encourage parent-child literacy interaction. When we incorporate cultural and linguistic identity in the classroom, we draw on students' "funds of knowledge" (Moll et al., 1994), the stores of information that all students bring to school. Our students' cultural knowledge and varied experiences will enrich the classroom environment. Unless students see themselves presented, promoted, and honored in the classroom, they will withdraw.

TEACHER DISPOSITIONS

A teacher's dispositions (see textbox 3.1) play a critical role in this learning process. In her research, Lisa Delpit (2012) defines features of a "warm demander," a term Castagno and Brayboy (2008) also reference as a key strategy for working with indigenous youth. According to Delpit, "warm demanders expect a great deal of their students, convince them of their own brilliance, and help them to reach their potential in a disciplined and structured environment" (p. 77). The teacher who is informal, caring, and capable of nurturing equity in the classroom captures key features of a warm demander.

While informal takes the shape of being playful or not overly serious, informal will not mean being indecisive or inconsistent. Students of all ages value fairness and consistency; they find comfort and familiarity in classroom routines. A routine helps to simplify a complex environment and to inform students exactly what to expect, what is expected of them, and what is acceptable behavior. With access to these expectations, youth will learn greater responsibility and will develop self-regulation. Furthermore, routines provide

TEXTBOX 3.1: TEACHER DISPOSITIONS

- Informal
- Caring
- Warm
- Authoritative without being authoritarian
- Respectful of all students
- Possessing a high expectation ethos
- Exhibiting the traits of a "warm demander"
- Appreciative of multiple cultures
- Recognizing the full potential of each student
- Providing challenges necessary for achieving that potential

predictability; with predictable patterns in place, teachers can spend more time in meaningful instruction.

Warm demanders not only believe in the potential of ALL students but also possess a high expectation ethos, holding students to a high standard of achievement while providing the scaffolds, accommodations, and modifications necessary for that achievement to occur. In this context, a scaffold is a form of temporary and adjustable support—like training wheels—that enables a learner to more readily and easily accomplish a task.

Conceptually similar, accommodations are supports that provide access to the curriculum content but do not fundamentally alter the learning goal or grade-level standard. Like eyeglasses or a distraction-free environment to complete a summative assessment, accommodations are essential because they enable students to participate fully in the instructional program and to complete essential learning tasks, although they may not be temporary.

Modifications, however, are changes to the curriculum and assessments that *do* fundamentally alter the learning goal or grade-level standard. These are often formalized and appear on a student's Individualized Education Plan (IEP). For example, the math teacher might modify the number of problems a student will complete. The critical difference to remember is that an accommodation affects HOW a student is learning and a modification affects WHAT a student is learning.

In holding students to rigorous standards, warm demanders are authoritative without being authoritarian. An authoritative style takes a supportive, flexible, assertive, and engaging approach to working with students. This individual—aware of the balance between support and control—sets limits and enforces consequences while using reason and appropriate negotiation. This leadership style that invites cooperation, empowers an adolescent's ability to make decisions and to solve problems, thereby developing self-regulation and self-confidence. Whereas the authoritarian might use verbal insults or dismiss another's feelings, the authoritative teacher nurtures and communicates reassurance.

To distinguish between the authoritarian and the authoritative teacher, consider the actions of Miss Trunchbull, the fictional headmistress of Crunchem Hall Primary School and one of the main antagonists in Roald Dahl's book *Matilda,* as authoritarian, and those of Miss Honey, Matilda's classroom teacher, as authoritative.

STUDENT DISPOSITIONS

Students often require reassurance when they forget that learning is a gradual process requiring time and effort. For them, understanding doesn't happen fast enough. They are surprised at their unknowing: "I don't understand," they will remark upon their initial encounter with Jonathan Swift's "A Modest Proposal" or their first attempt at doing a geometric proof. As novices, they don't yet know that the path to understanding is cluttered, digressive, and protracted; that understanding requires experience, dialectical practice, and intellectual habituation. An appropriate response to such impatience is "You're not supposed to understand. Not yet."

Those two words—Not Yet—send a subliminal message; they suggest promise and potential. *Potential,* with its root word *potent,* means that there is energy or force for growing, developing, and learning. Imagine the magic that might transpire if educators were to abolish the grades of D and F and replace them with NY—Not Yet. Instead of sending the demoralizing message of reprimand and failure, the NY suggests possibility—that given time, patient practice, and application, achievement will come. When a student says, "I don't get it" or "I can't do it," the nurturing "not yet" supports the notion of eventual competence (Miller, 2013).

To address bouts of student impatience, a teacher might produce a poster like the one in textbox 3.2 and hang it in the classroom to encourage students and to remind them that all learning is a gradual process that takes time and effort.

TEXTBOX 3.2: CLASSROOM POSTER

To understand, you have to think.
To think, you have to discover.
To discover, you have to learn.
Today, I want you to learn.
Tomorrow, we will assess what you've discovered;
then we will discuss what you think about it.
When we finish the process, you should understand.

After all, learning is not a passive act; it requires the consent and activity of the learner. In moments of confusion, students need the reminder that intelligence is not innate; it is developed through effort, motivation, and persistence in the face of struggle. They also need to know that brains are designed to change and grow.

This growth mindset (Dweck, 2010) enables the student to see struggle as an opportunity to demonstrate perseverance, even in the face of a daunting challenge. Teachers might invite students to develop a list of habits for effective learning. After brainstorming a list, the class can collaborate about the items they've listed, publishing the Top Ten Habits of Effective Learners, which may resemble those below. These lists serve as reminders to all students, who also need to:

- Establish goals and standards for performance
- Monitor progress during learning tasks
- Break complex problems/tasks into simpler components
- Allocate specific times to study and limit distractions while studying
- Take notes with attention paid to quality and quantity
- Outline material or organize learning tasks in explicit and concrete ways
- Monitor and attempt to control motivation and emotions (don't allow challenges or initial failure to deter progress)
- Identify and address obstacles, trying new approaches when necessary
- Ask questions and seek assistance and support when needed (build relationships with classmates, teachers, and other adults)
- Evaluate final outcomes and efforts, imposing consequences for performance

A second list might explore a recipe for success, naming the behaviors that define success. Success depends on:

- Following directions
- Completing assignments and submitting work on time
- Seeking out additional information or help
- Using rubrics or checklists to monitor performance
- Preparation for and investment in class activities
- Hope and learned optimism (believing I am the author of my own success story)
- Productive persistence—struggling through difficulty; fighting past the confusion
- Constructing meaning by actively interpreting, organizing, and applying new information
- Self-evaluating (looking over/checking work for accuracy)
- Repeatedly practicing material or using memory aids

Once published, these lists not only act as a common vocabulary for encouragement and confidence building but also support students in what psychologists call "attributional retraining" (Heider, 1958; Weiner, 1985).

SHAPING ATTITUDES

Attributional retraining (AR) is the process by which a person is led to reflect on his/her own attributions for a situation and to consider alternative explanations. For example, instead of thinking, "I'm not good at math or English," AR replaces unhelpful explanations about self-worth with attributions that will sustain self-esteem. A low grade or score doesn't imply lack of ability, but it does invite thinking about causes: Did I invest enough time in study/preparation or did I neglect to sufficiently prepare? Did I identify and address obstacles, trying new approaches when necessary, or did I give in to frustration, allowing the confusion to win?

Students need to know that a difficult test or topic may require different or more diligent test preparation strategies, seeking out help in a study buddy, or teacher conferencing.

According to attributional theorists, the causes students identify when accounting for their academic successes and failures will shape how they view their academic competence. Designed to enhance motivation and to encourage achievement, AR changes how students think so that their beliefs work for, rather than against, their chances for academic success. Students who feel they have some control over their academic success are more likely to recover from academic setbacks.

Two additional strategies for shaping attitudes are power posing and self-talk. Social scientist, Amy Cuddy (2010) and her team conducted research on body language and discovered that body position and posturing not only influence others but can cause neuroendocrine and behavioral changes that have powerful implications. Power posing for as little as two minutes induces elevations in testosterone and decreases in cortisol. With these hormone levels, individuals are psychologically and physiologically primed to be more assertive, confident, and relaxed. These increased feelings of power and decreased anxiety are precisely what we desire in high-stress environments, such as test taking or job interviews.

After reading the research report and watching Cuddy's TED Talk (2012) "Your Body Language May Shape Who You Are," a teacher might adapt and name four poses for demonstration. These four poses—Super Hero, Relaxed/Open, Aggressive Talker, and Boss—invite students to reshape their mindset. Anyone performing them for two minutes prior to a possibly stressful encounter will potentially be less reactive to stress and more likely to effectively handle a pressure situation.

This information can easily be shared with students during a Writing into the Day or Think About activity (see resource 3.1 at the end of this chapter) or by viewing the video as a class and conducting a text response. For example, in a lesson on how to write text summaries, a teacher might simply use this video text as a means to generate student response. Therefore, learners not only have the resources about power posing but a visual text for practicing the writing of a prized genre, the summary with its three movements: summarize, assess, and reflect (see textbox 3.3). A student written model of a text summary appears as resource 3.2 at the end of this chapter.

TEXTBOX 3.3: WRITING A TEXT SUMMARY

Think of the summary task as having three movements (not simply three paragraphs):

✓ *Summarize:* The first paragraph usually contains a *summary of the highlights of the text*. In your summary, include all the significant points of the work, including any points or features emphasized. Essentially, this section explains the purpose of the work and, if appropriate, the author's/designer's background and methodology. This summary should give a quick indication of the work's contents and your reaction to it. *Guiding Questions:* What is the main point, purpose, or goal of the text? What topics or message are conveyed? If someone asked what this resource features/offers, what would you say?

✓ *Assess:* Subsequent paragraphs typically explain and *evaluate the significance of the text*. Present your critical evaluation by discussing both positive and negative features as appropriate. Support all your judgments with evidence from the work, paraphrasing and quoting excerpts or giving detailed descriptions. *Guiding Questions:* Is the message useful? How does it compare with other messages? Is the information reliable? Is this information biased or objective? How effectively does the text meets its goal? Does it fill a void in the existing literature? Does it contain breakthrough information? Will it cause others in the field to revise their ideas about the subject? Conversely, is it just a rehash of previously known information? Is it well written/designed/conceived? Clear? Complete or missing important information? Is more research on the topic needed? Is the work thorough? fair? clear? convincing? significant? How does the work relate to other works in the field or to your general understanding of the subject?

> ✓ *Reflect:* Once you've summarized and assessed a source, you need to *reflect on how this text fits into your knowledge base.* Concluding paragraphs may make a recommendation about the type of reader likely to enjoy or benefit from the work and may include an indication of the work's merit in the field. *Guiding Questions:* Was this source helpful to you? How does it contribute to shaping your understanding? How can you use this source in your future work? How has it changed, advanced, or enlightened your thinking about this topic?

To accompany the power-posing exercise, teachers should introduce the power of positivity with self-talk. As students mirror the modeled poses, teachers encourage them to talk. While striking the Super Hero pose (feet planted shoulder width apart, shoulders squared, chest thrust out, chin up, and hands on hips—think Wonder Woman here), teachers might lead students to say with firm confidence, "I'm powerful; I dominate."

In the Relaxed/Open pose (sitting in a chair, butt a little forward, back resting, legs spread with one extended, arm up on the chair back), the exercise invites participants to say, in a relaxed and satisfying tone, "I've totally got this."

With the next pose, Aggressive Talker (standing behind a table with palms down and fingers somewhat extended as if about to spring, arms straight, leaning forward in an in-your-face posture), performers aggressively chant, "I won't stand for that kind of disrespect."

Finally, in the Boss pose (hands clasped behind our heads, shoulders relaxed and resting against the chair back, legs fully extended and crossed at the ankles with feet propped on a desk top if available), exercisers recite, "I'm large and in charge."

While the science of power posing has since been called into question, it represents the kind of self-talk that a teacher wishes to encourage. Considerable research does support the idea that people's beliefs about their abilities determine their chances of completing or not completing a task successfully.

Albert Bandura (1997) referred to this belief as self-efficacy, a critical aspect of motivation. Although countless factors contribute to this subjective and idiosyncratic notion, research conducted by Bandura and others confirms that self-efficacy plays a particularly provocative and influential role in initiating and sustaining engagement in an activity and that judging oneself as capable of success increases chances of actual success.

In this self-assessment process, verbal persuasion counts as influential, especially when delivered by a respected person like a teacher. An increase in student motivation comes from educators envisioning a student's success and articulating that vision for the student's aural benefit. If a writing teacher, for instance, expresses belief in an individual student's ability to acquire writing competence, the listener is likely to internalize that belief and to exert a corresponding effort.

Because research suggests that positive reinforcement provides significant motivation, assessment comments, then, should not only focus on correction or on developmental opportunities but also endorse successful moves, so as to honor ability and to offer encouragement. This praise can trigger another of the self-efficacy modalities, physiological-affective reaction. Elation, satisfaction, and gratification contribute to feelings of self-efficacy as readily as stress, humiliation, and regret. Although adolescents who struggle in learning situations will often ignore or discard praise as a trick to perform, that fact need not deter the warm demander who designs opportunities for students to find success. Students who experience success early and often are more likely to persist in future learning tasks.

LITERACY AND SELF-EFFICACY

Just as students bring a plethora of literate behaviors to a task, they bring a history of experiences that have shaped their perceptions of their abilities. Previous grade reports, teacher interactions, and parental and peer comments have all provided data from which the adolescent will draw to determine his/her identity as a learner. And these sources of self-efficacy are not easily overcome. Many students quickly decide that it is easier and less damaging to their self-esteems to say, "I won't" or "I don't want to" than to say, "I can't."

Still, frequent instructive and reinforcing feedback will do much to raise self-efficacy judgments and combat some of the aversive thoughts. According to Dweck (1986), the key to verbal persuasion lies in honoring effort, not intelligence. Attributing success to quantity and quality of effort results in enhanced self-efficacy since personal effort is within the individual's control, while intelligence and aptitude are considered more innate.

Yet, sharing positive comments alone will not produce the efficacy that educators seek. Specifically naming a successful move increases the likelihood of the student's repeating that rhetorical or problem-solving strategy and avoiding misapplication. Instead of vaguely saying, "Good job," a teacher might say, "Your participle strings effectively add movement and action to your description."

All of these strategies and methodologies seek to support and to scaffold learning, because when students perform in school-based settings, they are working outside their home discourses. Immersion in these new settings requires an expanded set of literate behaviors. Although literacy used to mean the ability to read and write, Street's (2001) "new literacy" view incorporates an array of social and cultural ways of knowing. His model draws attention to how people transform literacy to their own cultural concerns and interests. Not only an ability to navigate with language, literacy is a means of understanding one's world. In a sense, we wear our literacy like a skin—it identifies us, and we often value it for how it connects us.

This notion of identity and community also predominates in the work of James Gee (1989), who claims the focus of literacy studies should not be language but social practices. According to Gee, we humans all belong to discourse communities. In his definition, "a Discourse is a sort of 'identity kit' which comes complete with the appropriate costume and instructions on how to act, talk, and often write, so as to take on a particular role that others will recognize" (p. 6). Our primary discourse comes from our family and community, but as we grow beyond our homes, we develop secondary discourses.

A teacher can do much to nurture this literacy expansion and to develop these dispositions, and while key dispositions, ten habits, or four poses won't magically transform our classrooms, they do give us a place to start. Our dispositions reflect the beliefs we possess, beliefs which we live out in our actions, social involvement, and language—both aural and corporeal. Under the influence of these student and teacher dispositions, achievement is more likely to occur. After all, what we believe is not what we say; it's what we do. Our beliefs manifest in actions.

RESOURCE 3.1

Think Abouts and the Writer's Notebook

Think Abouts act as thinking serum. They generate ideas, prompt writing, and make visible our thinking so that it can be examined, reflected upon, and revised. By getting our ideas down quickly, we hopefully outrun our fearmongers and our internal critics and allow our own words to untangle our thoughts, an idea captured by British writer E. M. Forster when he asked: "How do I know what I think until I see what I say?" (Forster, 1927, pg. 101) Think Abouts are prompts meant to elicit deep thought about a social issue, interesting quote, or provocative question.

After experiencing a particular text, the class might take some reflection and rumination time during which they process their thoughts on the topic. Consequently, the response period for a Think About may consume three to five minutes. This rapid-response writing process helps writers generate ideas and get words on paper. This exercise also brings out the writer's voice, builds confidence, and develops fluency. Because Think Abouts are themselves "on-demand" writing topics, they foster the skills that students will need to perform in test situations; therefore, they act like test-prep materials, giving students the practice needed to think quickly and to record that thinking on paper.

However, Think Abouts aren't just for students. They allow all writers to write through questions, experiences, and imaginings. A teacher might use such prompts as a Writing into the Day ritual to make writing a habit of life. A Writer's Notebook serves as an idea bank or a safety deposit box where ideas can gather until such time as the author grows them into poems, articles, and personal essays.

After all, writing is thinking. When we write, we discover meaning in the world around us and in our own lives. A writing ritual such as this gives us the "imposed" time to pause and ponder. The resulting writing from a Think About is not meant to be a finished product, although teachers will likely hear writers share polished gems that reflect depth and beauty—proof that inside our heads, we have something valuable to say. Think Abouts provide the opportunity to dive in and experience the surprise and discovery that leads to new insight and knowledge.

During a Writing into the Day session in the classroom, teachers are encouraged to write along with their students. We might do this for many reasons, one of which can be selfish. As busy teachers, we often don't have the luxury of time to explore our thoughts or give ourselves permission to indulge in writing time beyond that required by our jobs. Yet, in writing we might find immense pleasure in twisting, twirling, and tinkering with words. We might rediscover that the writing craft is alive with possibility, discovery, and learning.

Writing with our students also reminds us how challenging and risky writing can be. Our struggles as writers can foster compassion and patience in our teaching. After a Writing into the Day session, the ritual of sharing our work aloud with the entire community or in small groups builds community. Because some writing is private, we will need to honor occasional requests to pass on sharing, as long as reticence is not a common choice.

The Writer's Notebook provides a chance for students to think and to write down their ideas so that we can honor their words and their voices, because what they say is poetry, and their thinking is discovery. Inside our heads, there lives a stream of feelings and remembrances and hurts and people and successful moments and colossal disappointments. Writing also hides in sweet learnings and epiphanies. By recording these thoughts, we can later dip into that stream of language; go fishing in the river of our minds and turn those ideas into more intentional writing. A teacher might invite students to expand an initial seed idea, growing a notebook prompt into a polished piece of writing—such as a poem or an essay for their course portfolios.

This practice of recording ideas and thoughts was at one time a popular way for civilized men and women to record striking passages they found in their reading. They kept what were called commonplace books. Who can forget the electrifying effect that some thoughts have on us when we encounter them for the first time? The commonplace book is a way of memorializing those striking passages so that one can return to them for renewed inspiration or for future reference—even as the seed for future writing.

Commonplacing is also the act or practice of entering lines, phrases, passages, and personal comments into a private journal, or, to use a seventeenth-century synonym, a *silva rerum* ("a forest of things"). Although Think Abouts themselves provide prompts for further thinking or reflection, teachers might encourage students to see their Writer's Notebook in this historical way.

Most professional writers keep such a notebook, a place where they can save words, phrases, golden lines, unrefined thoughts, and potential titles for a poem, essay, or song. Sometimes writers get their best ideas when they are away from their desks. Thus, the Writer's Notebook acts as a portable workbench. Writers return to their notebooks often to cultivate their insights. A teacher might encourage writers to think of their Writer's Notebook as a miniature greenhouse. By planting seeds and nurturing the ideas stored there, the results can reflect spectacular blossoms, perhaps a few weeds, and some marvelous mutations. With such a notebook, we can live in the world as writers—noticing, questioning, eavesdropping, observing, dreaming, and discovering.

Besides the power to spur thinking and writing, Think Abouts will potentially lead students to examine assumptions and prior knowledge, pose questions, make inferences, test interpretations, evaluate perspectives, find supporting evidence, respond to human behavior, imagine, and read like a writer. Students will continue to employ these core critical thinking strategies as adult citizens, whether in college, career, or community settings.

As students progress to eventually writing literary analyses or to writing in timed test settings, Think Abouts will have supplied the exploratory experience this new genre or style of questioning prompts. Their thinking will have practiced upward movement, providing a greater chance that their writing will also reflect greater depth and sharper focus.

Here is the protocol for doing a Think About:

- Write as quickly as you can for three to five minutes, recording whatever comes to mind in response to the prompt or topic; or

- Borrow a line or part of a line from the work and take that line for a walk; "taking a line for a walk" is a metaphor inspired by visual artist Paul Klee (1879–1940); or
- Use a specific line or particular style from the model provided and write an imitation or copy change of the original.

RESOURCE 3.2

Model of a Text Summary Written by a College Sophomore

Willis, J. (1999). *Susan Laughs*. New York: Henry Holt and Company.

In this book, readers meet Susan, who can do pretty much everything typical children can do, even though she is in a wheelchair. With assistance, Susan can perform physical activities like dancing and riding a horse. She also can be naughty, make mistakes, and experience emotions just like other children.

The cartoon-like drawings add interest to the book and create a sense that Susan is not different. In fact, the reader doesn't discover until the book's end that she is in a wheelchair. Pleasure comes from knowing that Susan is not confined to the wheelchair, which people often think is true. Willis's story dispels the stereotype that mobility impairment means a person can't do anything, when it might simply mean an inability to walk.

Maybe instead of making her cry and calling her weak, the creators of the book could have said she was sad about her math mistake. Otherwise the book is good.

I would use this book in the classroom because it shows that even though a person is in a wheelchair, that person can still do most everything and feel everything like everybody else can. The book assists readers in gaining accurate understanding of people with mobility impairments.

Chapter Four

Nurturing Social Justice

Whenever we observe human actions or behaviors, we have to remind ourselves that different cultural groups may react or behave in a manner that differs from our own. For example, just because someone dresses differently or exhibits unfamiliar mannerisms doesn't mean they are abnormal or wanting to draw attention to themselves. To see difference as a "freak flag" indicates the observer is looking from a biased lens. When we look without that bias, we can accept viable alternatives to our way of being in the world and be open to the possibility of difference.

For example, someone who cherishes his or her culture might make the sign of the cross when hearing an emergency vehicle's siren. This isn't weird behavior; it's a marker of faith. Just because someone lives in a community doesn't mean he/she needs to assimilate and adopt new practices and behaviors. For many cultures, that implies cultural suicide. The degree of acculturation will be determined by the individual. However, to live as a community will mean that we adapt to coexist and that we collaborate for harmony's sake. Author Debra Magpie Earling offers sage advice on this subject: "Honor your own beliefs, but also open your mind to the beliefs and perspectives of others."

Similar to Earling's advice, a teacher might remind students: "You might be entitled to your opinion, but you also have an obligation to decency." Young people especially like to spout their rights to their opinion and forget the value of a filter. As a result, teachers will likely need to remind students, "Just because an idea crosses your mind, doesn't mean it has to cross your lips."

Community living calls on its members to respect one another, and it is the teacher's responsibility to provide a safe and secure environment for all students, regardless of their cultural markers. Because we are stratified by our cultural attitudes, it is difficult to separate ourselves from them. So, when teachers hear harmful stereotypes or hurtful words, they are remiss if they ignore them or pretend deafness. As the lead adult in the room, it is the teacher's social responsibility to challenge parochial thinking, to intervene and interrupt hurt, and to provide information that might unseat whatever is keeping erroneous ideas in place.

PURSUING SOCIAL JUSTICE/TEACHING RESPECT

However, in pursuing justice, the teacher should consider the value in asking over judging or assuming: Why do you think that? Might there be another way to think? Or, the teacher might respond with statements like, I don't see the world that way. I invite you to imagine another way to see.

The acronym CEO provides an effective way to immediately bring to mind key intervention steps during breeches of social justice: *Call* the students on their remarks or behavior, *Explain* how the remark or behavior is hurtful, and *Offer* an opportunity for the individual to make amends—whether by apologizing or by admitting a commitment to new understanding (see textbox 4.1).

The CEO strategy is modeled after the "three-tier approach" developed by educational consultant and author Abe Louise Young (2011). The approach offers a method for dealing with prejudicial comments in the classroom and for increasing the likelihood for positive change. Since these steps can be difficult to remember spontaneously—especially under circumstances where emotion has escalated—teachers might consider posting them in the room as a reminder for engendering ally behavior. This tiered approach allows educators to tell the truth and to ensure that all parties are reasonably protected while also communicating the clear message that hate speech/behavior is not accepted in the classroom.

TEXTBOX 4.1

Call the students on their remarks or behavior

Explain how the remark or behavior is hurtful

Offer an opportunity for the individual to make amends

Having an easy-to-recall solution such as this when emotions might otherwise cloud judgment is critical in teaching. The acronym further sends a subliminal message to the teacher: as the chief executive officer, the highest-ranking person in the classroom, you are ultimately responsible for providing leadership and serving as a role model. In their classrooms, teachers frequently seek to create a microcosm of the world in which they wish to live. If we encounter prejudice, do we intervene and interrupt hurt, do we create conditions that reduce instances of injustice, or do we remain silent?

This topic calls to mind Anna Sewell's declaration in *Black Beauty*: "With cruelty and oppression, it is everybody's business to interfere when they see it" (p. 106). Pastor Martin Niemöller's words upon his release from Dachau also come to mind:

First, they came for the socialists, and I did not speak out—because I was not a socialist.

Then they came for the trade unionists, and I did not speak out—because I was not a trade unionist.

Then they came for the Jews, and I didn't speak out—because I was not a Jew.

Then they came for me—and there was no one left to speak for me. (qtd. in Gerlach, 2012, p. 47)

Many of us want to be someone who speaks up because we know the pain of hurtful taunts and can imagine how abandoned and alone someone might feel when under attack. Empathy building demands that we be brave, be fair, and be kind. Teachers need strategies that are honest and inclusive, strategies for interrupting prejudice and social injustice, strategies that move away from Anglo-centrism without vilifying Anglos.

After all, there is a difference in feeling guilty and taking responsibility. Mutual respect cannot arise from ignorance. We confront the truth and then work for social justice, ensuring that all parties are reasonably protected. With such philosophies that honor difference and build empathy, and with strategies like the CEO approach and the Sharing Circle discussed in chapter 2, teachers build trust, teach respect, and promote a sense of community.

Teaching respect might begin by looking from another's perspective, by imagining another way to see, and by accepting multiple truths. For example, one culture, such as the Choctaw Indian, may see the owl as a foreshadowing of death or imminent harm; another culture might perceive of the owl as a symbol of wisdom. Cultural subtleties like these emerge every day.

Consider this shopper's experience: A consumer had selected a chunk of sliced ham whose price rang up at $6.66, and the clerk asked the customer whether she wanted to go select another ham. The shopper respectfully replied that 666 was just a number until the clerk assigned an alternate meaning to it. The clerk's reality was that 666 was the devil's number. Although the devil may be in the details, the customer still bought the ham.

Reflecting on the foregoing interaction might remind a person that being cognizant of and sensitive to subtle differences reflects a culturally responsive mindset. That transaction confirmed that there are many ways of seeing. Each has an element of truth, but none is the whole truth. If we limit ourselves to one way of seeing, to one truth, we will limit our power. Competent thinking calls for flexibility and a willingness to learn from different sources. We enrich our knowledge base by examining multiple perspectives, researching different ways of knowing, and accepting that personal understanding and experiences provide a limited viewpoint.

TAKING STOCK OF AND CONFRONTING BIAS

When teachers encourage students to wonder about their preferences and to consider their biases, that reflective process will often produce learning. Those who reflect may realize that focusing on their way, their idea, their belief as the best limits their ability to learn about anything else. Without a thorough, balanced approach to knowledge acquisition, our learning is tragically incomplete. After all, an alternate opinion isn't necessarily wrong; it might simply be different.

As we encounter new truths and research different ways of knowing, those truths are always incomplete. Besides admitting that we can never know all there is to know, we must accept that all incoming data is refracted and discolored by the prism of our own personal understanding and experiences. These facets reflect a limited viewpoint. Rather than reject alternate opinions as faulty notions or as anomalies that lie too far out of our frame of reference, we can allow diversity to enhance our knowledge base.

To encourage this form of thinking, teachers might introduce students to what is sometimes referred to as the Busy Intersection Method, although some call it the Four Corners Method. Using this protocol invites individuals to picture a city intersection where four streets intersect. Traffic snarls at such intersections, and crashes are more likely to occur. Such is also the case with multiple perspectives and the prospect of clashing opinions.

The Busy Intersection Method is a way of viewing a topic. We all have different lenses that we look through when considering a topic. Our lenses are influenced by our gender, religion, ethnicity and race, socioeconomic status, name/family, age, place, perception of belonging, language, and exceptionality.

All of these influences shape our beliefs and behaviors. In fact, they affect not only *what* but *how* we see; experience colors perception. For instance, we all probably have a viewpoint about European colonization. A white, middle-class American's notion of this event will likely differ from that of a Japanese American, Native American, Jewish American, or LGBTQ American. Unique perspectives grow out of our previous experiences. Because we bring our beliefs and previous experiences to every new data encounter, we create a busy intersection for discussion. Even though we share the same incident, we no doubt have a different story to tell.

Designing a graphic organizer, students can select one incident, name four (or more) diverse perspectives, and then explain how each perspective changes the truth that a particular person "sees." From such an exercise, students not only discover how those differences impact reliability, they also encounter the notion of multiple truths and how sometimes we need all four stories to determine what *really* happened. Just as a busy intersection commands, with difficult conversations we must exercise patience, respect certain "traffic laws," and yield when necessary.

In response to social injustices, some groups will attack and criticize the aggressor; those responses are initial strategies in taking back power lost in oppressive situations. The consequences of colonization and conquest continue today, whether we look to situations in Guatemala, Israel, Palestine, or Indian Country. The ensuing violence or critical responses in these conflicts derive from the hurt and anger the oppressed endure. As teachers, we don't want to criticize, but we do want to tell the truth. We also want to show where hope is growing.

Allowing stereotypes to percolate to the surface for examination has the potential for heated debate as well as for healing. We cannot allow guilt to be the glue that holds prejudice in place, nor can we focus on finger pointing and blaming.

MAKING ROOM FOR NEW LEARNING

Sometimes the conflict resides in the difference between willingness and willfulness. Are we willing to let go of the pain, to extend apology or forgiveness, to allow someone else to share our privileged place, or do we willfully cling to convictions, tradition, and the status quo? Both sides of any argument will be guilty of harboring biases. We naturally cast something in our own light—based on our experiences or cultural values—often unaware of our blindness, our parochial notions that exclude other ways of knowing.

This is not to imply that we let go of what we believe, but we do need to be curious about what someone else believes, to imagine another way to see. Our knowledge isn't the only truth, and we don't live in a binary world where something is strictly right or wrong, good or evil, mysterious or meaningful, male or female. Even though our brains crave the clarity of a world that unfolds in a straight line, much of life is lived in the gray areas and follows a circuitous path upon which we may meet gender-fluid individuals who identify as multiple choice on a true-false test.

In our search to reconcile these disparities, there is no easy solution. The word *solution* suggests that a complex issue like racism is fixable, but maybe we have gone beyond fixing; the sky has fallen, and the issue now is how to take care of one another. Maybe all we can do is apply compassion and work one child at a time. When we choose to be a change agent or an ally, we focus on how we can build common ground or how we can unite conflicting viewpoints. Consider the individual's personal role: When I stand in the middle, I help to unite; when I step aside, I watch opportunity for community untie and unravel.

Sometimes, the best that teachers can do is create the world in their classroom where they want to live, one where they can help students to find their power and to have confidence.

As we nurture social justice, it is important to remember that cultural crafts hung in a classroom are only part of a people's culture. Culture is more than heroes and holidays and more than costumes and cuisine. These trappings often capture the "ideal" rather than the "real" culture that is lived day by day through that group's language, family kinships, and social networks. What a culture values and believes and what they consider as meaningful experience may not be represented in these perceived symbols.

Certainly, cultural crafts like music, dance, cuisine, and holiday motifs are integral to all cultures because they unite people; they are rooted in the meaning of people's real culture. However, when we spotlight only the visible ideal, we make way for stereotypes—either exoticizing or minimizing people's real-life, complex experiences. In that, we must proceed with caution.

Although culture will enter the classroom or workplace in many ways, it will manifest in behaviors. It is equally important not to stereotype children's behavior. Often, teachers will judge misbehavior as defiance, disrespect, low ability, or disinterest when it may be an indicator for either difficulty or boredom with simplicity. In some cultures, silence or downcast eyes are forms of respect, so insisting upon eye contact or a verbal response may work counter to culture.

Given cultural differences, we will want to be cautious about discipline—avoiding assumption, judgment, belittling, or raising our voices. We can be firm and frame rules in a positive expectation-explicit form: "I want to see everyone quietly putting away materials." Setting high expectations, providing lessons that don't rely too heavily on competition, and paying special attention to how meritocracy and individualism operate in classrooms are essential considerations in building a culturally responsive environment, one that promotes social cooperation, justice, and ethical practices.

Multiple lessons are available in a children's book described by its author as "two nursery rhymes with pictures." *We Are All in the Dumps with Jack and Guy* by Maurice Sendak (1993) records evidence of social injustice as well as evidence of noble actions to set right a world gone rotten. Sendak illustrates how a gesture of kindness multiplies. When Guy says of the little brown-complexioned boy, "Let's buy him some bread," like magic, a monstrous white cat appears and attacks the rats, rescuing the kids and the kittens. When white Guy befriends the little dark boy, even against the wishes of Jack, soon Jack, too, reforms—realizing that love, not hatred, is what the world needs; rescue, not destruction. Authors like Sendak offer us a reason to hope for social justice. Random acts of kindness can repair the rent in our social fabric.

Socioeconomic class is socially constructed by society and its institutions, and Sendak seems to suggest that we all share the dilemma of rectifying that construction through reconstruction, not destruction. While none of us can "help" the fact that we were born into a particular family, place, or socioeconomic strata, we might consider how we can reform the political and social systems that try to keep us there—if we are trapped or if we do in fact endure conditions we wish to overcome. Rather than blaming the disadvantaged, we need to consider ways to provide access to alternatives, to combat the inequities, to think about how we might allow others to be in the place of power and privilege that some enjoy.

In the classroom, that means the curriculum does not only reflect the perspective of middle-class America. It also implies we are cognizant of socioeconomics and cautious about assumptions. Not every student has access to the resources many of us take for granted. A project that requires a computer or even colored pencils might present a disadvantage to some.

One parent recalled when her son was in high school and students were required to buy TI-83 programmable calculators. In 2003, they cost nearly $100.00, and this mother knew not every one of her son's peers' families could afford that sum, but it's also embarrassing for a student who has to use one of the school's calculators. When that happens, we call attention to someone else's poverty.

While there may be no easy solution to that dilemma, some parents sacrifice deeply to provide for their children. Teachers can step in to help. Providing class time and making the supplies and resources available to all is one path; reaching out to underrepresented families is another.

Teachers cannot expect working-class, culturally diverse families to reject their culture and fit into a mainstream culture. Instead, teachers adopt positive attitudes toward differences, recognizing the complexity of people, their lives, and interests. A certain lifestyle is what we know. To suggest that those beliefs or ways of being in the world are wrong or need to be escaped is problematic. To insinuate that family conditions or the people at home are holding students back pits one way against another. The goal is to orient the learning setting to equitably serve the students of ALL cultures, not just the dominant culture.

To reach that goal, teachers often adopt the belief that all can achieve and that no one culture is higher or lower, greater or lesser than any other. Teachers create settings where classroom content is relevant and reflects diversity. They organize content around interdisciplinary or cross-curricular themes that scaffold students' learning, because the research shows that those methods increase access to achievement.

Teachers might also design learning modules that support student participation in completing tasks otherwise beyond their reach. The degree to which students value academic activities and whether they see realistic purposes to motivate them are influential in determining their participation. Such activity engagement often begins with motivation. Activating that switch to positively impact student learning might involve giving students significant topics to discuss.

Another title for inspiring social action and for inviting us to examine our own stereotypes is *Seedfolks* by Paul Fleischman (1997). In sixty-nine pages, Fleischman creates a tapestry of culture, showing the power of social action and community camaraderie. Like a plush and colorful Persian rug, the Gibb Street Garden weaves the cultural threads of Southern blacks and whites, Vietnamese, Polish, European, Guatemalan, Puerto Rican, Jewish, Haitian, Korean, British, Mexican, and Indian community members all living in Cleveland.

An additional text for doing this important work is Tony Hoagland's "America" (2003), a poem of social consciousness that comments on contemporary American society. An ensuing discussion may focus on the poem's sensory language (*gushed, spilling, clogging*), its use of specific brand names to represent contemporary consumerism (*Radio Shacks, Burger Kings, MTV episodes*), its conversational and informal tone intermixed with rich figurative language (*And as I consider how to express how full of **it I think he is; And I remember what Marx said near the end of his life*), and its form (the poem, told in eighteen unrhymed couplets, is one long interrogative question).

Those dialogically engaged, however, will likely address not only what the poem says, but what it means, and why that meaning matters. Perhaps they would conclude that the poem examines how Americans often use material things and other distractions to drown out those who are suffering as a consequence of society's ills. Perhaps they would evaluate what has been lost as a result of the efficiency of fast food, remote control, and satellite speed downloads. Such a conversation might lead to a discussion about Marshall McLuhan, who is considered by many to be the first father and leading prophet of the electronic age and who spent his career attempting to understand and explain the effects of technology as it related to popular culture.

In a college course preparing teachers to teach Oral Language and Media Literacy, instructors have used the prompt: *We Americans have fallen in love with technology and digital tools, but consider for a moment how technology might hinder, rather than enhance, learning.* That prompt led to an extensive discussion of Marshall McLuhan's media criticism, as well as to an exploration of the invasive and pervasive techniques of American advertising.

During further reflection on this topic, a person may recall the words of Kappelman (2002), who said that "every extension of mankind, especially technological extensions, have the effect of amputating or modifying some other extension. An example of an amputation would be the loss of archery skills with the development of gunpowder and firearms" (p. 3). McLuhan believed that mankind has always been fascinated and obsessed with these extensions, but too frequently we choose to ignore or minimize the amputations. Flooded by technology and enjoying the luxuries it provides, we have lost our fear; we have forgotten stories like Ray Bradbury's (1951) "The Veldt," which warns that "Happylife Home" with its superfluous technological gadgetry can kill us.

In an effort to give a more scientific basis to his theories and his work, in later years, McLuhan developed a concept called the *tetrad*. This *tetrad* allowed McLuhan to apply four laws, framed as questions, to a wide spectrum of mankind's endeavors, essentially providing a useful tool for examining our culture:

- What does it (the medium or technology) extend?
- What does it make obsolete?
- What is retrieved?
- What does the technology reverse into if it is over-extended?

Applying McLuhan's tetrad might force us to think critically about and to uncover the hidden consequences of the technologies we develop.

Most students concluded that McLuhan would probably agree with today's researchers who suggest, if the tool enhances teaching and learning, it is worth using. If it does not, then we might explore how it might actually hinder learning. It is remarkably easy for tools like Smart Boards, computers, iPads, and smart phones to become the focus of education rather than the content. In this context, especially given the amount of time young people devote to electronic devices (5,000 text message per month, claim 2018 statistics), we might do well to remember both the extensions and the amputations.

Hoagland's poem works effectively as a Writing into the Day exercise for a group of students, especially if they have previously been taught a technique called "taking a line for a walk." This metaphor was inspired by visual artist Paul Klee (1879–1940) who described drawing as "simply a line going for a walk."

Drawing on this analogy, writing workshops use the method to spark critical thinking, writing, and discussion. After reading or hearing a song, poem, or other text, writers choose from the text a line that strikes them, copies it, and then continue in their own words, letting that line lead their thinking. The strategy illustrates the power of spontaneity. After hearing Hoagland's poem, one student focused on the line "The thick satin quilt of America," and wrote:

> While "the thick satin quilt of America" provides images of comfort and luxury and warmth, it also has the power to suffocate. The poet's focus on luxury as a tool for destruction shocks me. But it's true that we use stuff and noise to drown out the suffering of others, of those who might need our help. We insulate ourselves from their cries. We silence the cries of the desperate, the impoverished, the needy with "things." Consumerism is the culprit since we have learned to love things instead of people. Unless we shift our priorities, it seems America is in trouble.

Using contentious topics like Hoagland's poem as catalysts for sparking conversations on complex social issues, we raise social consciousness and support collaborative conversation. O'Donnell-Allen (2011) and Davis (2012) also encourage contentious topics as a method for teaching civil discourse and making a difference in the world. Students who experience opportunities to openly discuss what's awry about the society in which they live, to read a text as social protest literature, or to develop a body of knowledge about contemporary social conditions and to critically examine the culture that created those conditions develop civic awareness, critical thinking skills, and argument literacy.

With these analysis, argument, and public conversation skills, we give students access to forms of intellectual capital that have power in both the corporate and the academic worlds. These skills also provide access for those wishing to enter political and social conversations as they vie for resources or rally to promote positive change. A thinking, democratic populace should possess the skills necessary for interrogating social and political practices and policies.

THE ROLE OF CULTURAL IDENTIFY LITERATURE

Cultural Identity Literature (CIL) also has potential to positively impact student learning. It motivates readers because it features characters and issues adolescent readers can readily identify with; the texts are relevant and relatable. A springboard for stimulating critical thinking and engagement, CIL provides the opportunity to read, to write, and to argue about social issues in a modern context. Generally, English and social studies teachers don't just want students to read novels; they want to expose them to multiple perspectives, to situations that encourage a critical stance so as to inspire wisdom that might lead to an improved way of living in the world. But without the relevance factor, youth won't remain interested and invested.

As teachers try to balance reading as an act of pleasure and reading as a tool for increasing academic prowess in their students, they might look to what Don Gallo (2008) called *bold books*. According to Gallo, these are the best books because they deal in the gray areas of life. Although these books are often targeted as controversial, Gallo says, "Good books have always caused people to think, and since few of us think alike, controversy is guaranteed" (p. 116). Bold books provide the primer for living life, "and there's no better place to explore the larger, diverse, often scary world than from the safe distance a book provides" (p. 117).

The bold books listed in textbox 4.2 explore the topic of bullying and invite contentious talk on an important social issue.

These books not only reveal the egregious consequences of bullying but offer models for intervention at school, where adolescents often experience divisive roles based on cultural markers like class, gender, and race—qualities that confer social capital on some and marginalize others.

Conversations about tough topics like bullying are necessary to the growth and learning of students since talking is a road to understanding. Reading texts that feature tough topics not only imparts information but also assists readers in forming opinions after encountering multiple perspectives. Using a text like Sendak's picture book, Hoagland's poem, or any other bold text as a tool for tough talk further affords conversants some distance from the topic, which can be filtered through a character's reaction or opinion.

TEXTBOX 4.2: BOLD BOOKS ON THE TOPIC OF BULLYING

The Absolutely True Diary of a Part-Time Indian, Sherman Alexie (Little, Brown, 2007)
The Bully, Paul Langan (Townsend Press, 2002)
The Chocolate War, Robert Cormier (Pantheon, 1974)
The Hunger Games, Suzanne Collins (Scholastic, 2008)
King of the Screwups, K. L. Going (Harcourt, 2009)
Nineteen Minutes, Jodi Picoult (Atria, 2007)
Okay for Now, Gary D. Schmidt (Clarion Books, 2011)
Party, Tom Leveen (Random House, 2010)
Plague Year, Stephanie Tolan (HarperTrophy, 1999)
Speak, Laurie Halse Anderson (Farrar, Straus & Giroux, 1999)
Schooled, Gordon Korman (Hyperion, 2007)
Sweetgrass Basket, Marlene Carvell (Dutton Children's Books, 2005)
Stargirl, Jerry Spinelli (Knopf, 2000)
Taking Sides, Gary Soto (Sandpiper, 2003)
Tangerine, Edward Bloor (Harcourt, 1997)
Thirteen Reasons Why, Jay Asher (Razorbill, 2007)
Twisted, Laurie Halse Anderson (Viking, 2007)
Wringer, Jerry Spinelli (HarperTeen, 2004)

This attribution provides a level of safety for adolescents who are still discovering their own identities and forming individual philosophies. It can also provide a level of safety for the teacher who is allowing the authors to ask the difficult questions.

Other texts with potential for nurturing social justice and for encouraging critical thinking include spoken word poems like "Tamara's Opus" by Joshua Bennett and "S for Lisp" by George Watsky. In a performance at the White House Evening of Poetry, Music, and the Spoken Word on May 12, 2009, Brave New Voices slam champion Bennett chastises himself for not destroying the communication barricade with his sister who is deaf and apologizes for being unwilling to learn sign language until his adult life.

Although both poet performances are readily available on YouTube, the Watsky poem, which was performed at the 2010 Collegiate National Poetry Slam Finals, might not be appropriate for all contexts and audiences, as it does have some mature scenes and language. Still, poems such as these have power to influence the human condition. With their tapestry of sound and thematic richness, we can claim a voice out of the silence.

While both poems honor those who are differently able, in his performance, Watsky renders his critics impotent by reclaiming his confidence in his speech and ability to communicate. Watsky's performance works effectively as a prewriting activity in an upper-level secondary school classroom or a college writing course as students prepare to write rants (see textbox 4.3). After writing their responses to Watsky's performance, the class discussed how some human behaviors or social flaws make our blood boil. To further prepare for their rant writing, the class read several more rant models with an eye towards knowing they would be creating a piece of writing like this.

TEXTBOX 4.3: RANTS

For this essay (two to four pages with research, if needed) you can choose to rage, rant, and complain (using humor, perhaps?) about something that really sticks in your craw or royally irritates you. This may be the prevalence of text speak, the annoyance of pop-up ads, someone's naive belief in multitasking, or the pervasive retelling of blonde jokes.

To kick off the semester, you will use a claim and supportive evidence to build your rant. Most crucial in this sort of essay is your voice as a writer and your ability to get "buy-in" from the audience. After all, anger can be transformed into beneficial civic action.

For maximum impact, couch your rant or rampage within a good story, one featuring vivid descriptive passages. Your goal is not simply to complain but to share a viewpoint or to present an argument that others may neglect to notice. So that your tirade leads to insight, you need to paint a full picture, by providing plenty of context and by backing up your viewpoint with a scenic truth. To do this, the reader must either "identify with the narrator" (you) or accept your ranting as a part of the writer's idiosyncratic wisdom.

During the students' inquiry of these models, as they determine how such writing performs, a teacher might encourage the writers to notice what makes each essay effective, listing any rhetorical strategies they found peculiar to the rant genre. Guiding questions can further scaffold student learning:

- What strategies do the authors use that seem to differ from other writing?
- Examine word choice—what kinds of words get used?

- Examine sentence structure or patterns—what do you notice?
- Examine tone—how does the writer develop tone?
- What are the common tones in this genre?

Once they have thoroughly evaluated and discussed the rant genre, students are typically ready to write their own rants. Finished pieces can be read during Read-Around Groups, a peer revision protocol where writers assess one another's writing for the features discovered during inquiry (see resource 4.1 at the end of this chapter). Writers who have this kind of investment in the writing process—naming significant strategies and then producing them—are often more empowered to write.

The "in your face" approach with Watsky's *s*-inundated performance empowers him and reduces the labeled criticisms—lisp, handicap, and speech defect—to mere misnomers. These are the kinds of confidence lessons we teachers hope to give our students; we don't want to be guilty of having a listening impediment. When we help students to find their power, to have confidence, when we honor their "funds of knowledge," we give them access to their ability; we become literacy sponsors.

This sponsorship begins with paying attention, with listening, so that we can discern the learning styles and strengths of our students and then guide them to uncover their own knowledge. Our focus shouldn't be on covering curriculum material but on supporting our students in discovering their literacies and using those strengths for uncovering their cognitive power.

Another accessible text is Susan Boyle's first audition on the TV show *Britain's Got Talent*. Even for those who have seen it before, watching Boyle's jaw-dropping performance is the kind of fairy tale moment that engenders goose bumps. To those individuals who work with young people, this video is a reminder to never pre-judge or allow prejudiced attitudes to color perceptions but instead to always believe in possibility, to nurture and sponsor a student's literacy in whatever area he/she displays passion. Just because someone doesn't appear polished doesn't mean that individual doesn't have talent or ability. Such moments serve as a reminder that we all of us have gifts, we just open them at different rates.

In addition, Boyle's performance reminds us how people are swayed pretty easily by something attractive—a slick presentation, a glitzy advertisement, a catchy or sophisticated message, even a model's figure or face. Barry Lyga's book *Hero-Type* (2008) addresses this theme, while also exploring what it means to be a hero, to support convictions, to preserve freedom, and to exercise patriotism.

Lyga goes one step further by addressing the power of words and revealing how people—like politicians or advertisers—manipulate the populace: "If you make a complicated message simple, you can get a lot of people on your side, even if you're wrong and even if it's not true" (p. 163)—scary thought, but true. People tend to be swayed by charisma, and where one goes, often others follow.

This power of words is one of the most important lessons we can give our students. Just as words can manipulate and seduce, they can also open our eyes, our minds, and our imaginations. We can also use words to open ourselves to new ways of thinking, feeling, and being.

Hoping to give students a visual of how the act of daring to do something differently may hold beauty, a teacher might demonstrate with an apple. Asking a group what method is considered typical for cutting an apple in half will likely produce the response: Cutting from the top (stem end) to the bottom (blossom end). Asking what may happen if a person instead decides to cut an apple in half at its middle, perpendicular to that imaginary line, might produce a surprising outcome. After making the cut and seeing the resulting star inside, observers might recognize that stepping outside of our comfort zones can sometimes produce beautiful results.

This exercise contributes to the class' common vocabulary, and from that point on, whenever someone uses the statement "Find the star," they will know it is a reminder to step outside their comfort zones or to broaden their minds.

With relevant and authentic topics, educators provide opportunities for students to engage in reflective processes that include dialogue, writing, inquiry, and other metacognitive activities. These rich, reflective components integrate the critical thinking skills prized by the Common Core Standards and essential to raising social consciousness.

Because writing develops critical thinking in ways that foster reconsideration and transformation, writing topics that are tailored to the students in the room are often more engaging. For a group of high school seniors, a teacher might invite writing about the social practice of memorializing virtue and to consider who gets left out in these commemorations.

With the Captured in Stone research project (see resource 4.2 at the end of this chapter), students often write convincing essays that argue for alternate images in a "new" Mount Rushmore. This National Memorial located in the Black Hills of southwestern South Dakota currently features colossal sculptures of the heads of U.S. presidents George Washington, Thomas Jefferson, Abraham Lincoln, and Theodore Roosevelt. One of the first questions the group may ask is "Where are the women?"

This authentic student question sparks a history lesson. Recall that chapter 1 of this book pointed out that art is a cultural encyclopedia, that to learn about a time period or to catch a glimpse of a people's values and beliefs, scholars need simply look to the art from that period. In 1927 when the Mount Rushmore project was initiated, women had only recently obtained the right to vote and the United States was still focused on the patriarchy. Some would say it still is. American founders—Anti-Federalists and Federalists alike—considered rule by majority "a troubling conundrum," according to Eric Chenoweth (2016) who writes for Democracy Web.

While majority rule may be necessary as a means for making decisions and for ensuring that when decisions are made, more people are in favor than opposed, preventing injustice is nearly impossible. Because statesman James Madison was concerned about such dangers and wished to provide protections against oppression, he drafted the Bill of Rights, which were adopted as the first Ten Amendments to the U.S. Constitution, with intentions to guard one faction of society against the injustice of the other.

Although the idea of minority rights was discussed early in American history as protection from political tyranny, minority rights—those rights granted to act as a safeguard of minority interests and help prevent discrimination against them by the majority—didn't become a serious part of the political lexicon until after World War I when minority rights' protection was for the first time formally included in the international legal framework through the League of Nations' Minority Treaties.

Despite all of the political efforts, activism, and policies on the subject of civil and political rights, discrimination persists today, along with the question: How can minority groups be guaranteed political and social representation within a democratic framework? Educators can conduct these important conversations so that unifying and positive language can someday replace the divisiveness we currently experience in the United States.

A repurposed version of the Captured in Stone project also found its way into a college writing course at a tribal college in North Central Montana (see resource 4.3 at the end of this chapter) to inspire critical thinking and to practice research writing skills. Personalizing the topic to the audience of students not only considers context but maximizes relevance and student agency.

Relevance and agency are words we hear often in the educational arena. Although they may seem like the new buzzwords, they are not just fashionable expressions. Learning will not happen without them. Students are more likely to stay in school, learn, and achieve at high levels if they find the curriculum relevant to and compatible with their own cultural values, life experiences, and personal needs.

Pedagogies that offer real-life learning from which students find meaning produce student agency. Student agency refers to empowering students through curriculum approaches that:

- engage them
- are respectful of and seek their opinions
- give them opportunities to feel connected to school life
- promote positive and caring relationships between all members of the school community
- promote well-being and focus on the whole student
- relate to real-life experiences
- are safe and supportive.

Educational systems increase the likelihood of relevance with curriculum when what happens in school holds significance outside of school or counts for something in peer group interaction or beyond school. When we inventory student interests and welcome them in the classroom, we increase relevance and agency. From the point where school-based literacies intersect with community literacies, those interested in responsive teaching can extract important information about issues of agency and about the value of relevance.

In these times of shifting literacy demands, educators are poised to implement pedagogical principles that will develop student agency. We can achieve agency with curricular designs that meet learners where they live, honoring and incorporating their multiple discourses and recognizing the importance of motivation and youth representation in school-based literacies. In the absence of such focus, many schools and teachers risk disengagement due to student feelings of irrelevance and disempowerment.

These processes of developing empowerment and agency will also extend to helping writers understand that writing is hard work. Fostering this belief will prepare writers to see their struggle as part of the writing process and not as a sign of their own inadequacy. If the classroom culture has taught them to view writing as a valuable activity and as one in which the work is separate from the self, writers are less likely to experience shame when they receive corrective feedback or suggestions for revision from either peers or the teacher.

Finding that balance where writers possess a healthy separation from their writing yet maintain a vested interest in it will be a challenge, but it comes with teaching writers to accept failure as part of the learning process and finding ways to honor struggle, a topic discussed in chapter 3.

The projects in this chapter that address social inequity and injustice empower students to explore which identities are privileged or denied, affirmed or suppressed. Writing about and discussing these issues not only builds awareness but cultivates an empathetic citizenry. Educators can pose the questions and support the students in their slogging for answers or students can ask their own questions and seek out answers as the teacher nurtures and nudges.

While some of these conundrums will have no easy answers, educators can enflame a commitment to ongoing learning and progress toward a more nearly perfect world. When we challenge students to live up to expectations of being supportive of rights for all people, they will often rise to the challenge. These mental experiences not only help students think differently about their worlds, they also help them to behave differently. Because when we change the way we see, we often change who we are.

RESOURCE 4.1

Read-Around Protocol for Rants

Subject of the Rant/Focus of Criticism: _____

_____

(Place a ✓ on the line to indicate acceptable/proficient; place a plus + for advanced/creative ability; or insert a minus – to indicate nearing proficiency.) The author sets out to illustrate this focus with

- Concrete Examples/Detail/Quotations _____

- Strong Tone _____. Identify it below (i.e. harsh, smart-assy, caustic, emphatic, humorous) _____

- Flowing Patterns (maybe long/short) _____

- Vivid Language/Loaded Words (sometimes expletives) _____

- Sarcasm _____

- Reader Engagement (personal and conversational) _____

- Questions (often rhetorical) _____

My favorite part of the paper: _____

_____

My most significant suggestion for improvement: _____

_____

I (circle one) did/did not sense a strong voice in the author's style as he/she attempted to stir me to action.

Peer Reviser's Signature: _____

RESOURCE 4.2

Captured in Stone—Research Topic

Background: Mount Rushmore, the National Memorial located in the Black Hills of southwestern South Dakota, features colossal sculptures of the heads of U.S. presidents George Washington, Thomas Jefferson, Abraham Lincoln, and Theodore Roosevelt. The four were chosen to represent, respectively, the nation's founding, philosophy, unity, and expansion. Artist Gutzon Borglum designed and oversaw construction of the monument, a project which spanned 1927–1941.

Topic: If the federal government or some other benefactor were ever to fund a similar project, whose likeness would merit the time enduring honor of being captured in stone? Deliberate and establish a set of criteria you will use in determining probable candidates, then measure your choices against this list of requirements. Use research to validate your final selection. Write persuasively to convince the audience of the appropriateness of your contestant's virtues.

Organization: You might consider an introduction that discusses the possibility and significance of another monument like Mount Rushmore and the challenges you faced in choosing likely nominees. In another paragraph, outline and define the criteria an individual had to meet to qualify for consideration. Who were your finalists, and how did you finally name your winner? In subsequent paragraphs based on research and personal opinion, provide evidence of accomplishments and achievements that testify to your personality's qualifications for such a prodigious memorial. Conclude with a final paragraph regarding the historical, social, philosophical, cultural, or political value of such a memorial and restate this candidate's worth.

Additional Criteria: You must read at least one biography about your chosen person's life and use this as your primary source. Include at least two other sources, preferably five total, to lend depth to your research and development to your report. Also, include a bibliography labeled Works Cited.

Works Cited Page: A Works Cited page in MLA style is an alphabetical list of all the sources cited in writing your research paper. Prepare this page using the following tips:

- The Works Cited page is numbered and is always the last page of your paper.
- Entries are listed under the centered heading Works Cited.
- Entries are listed alphabetically and double spaced.
- Each new entry begins at the left margin. Additional lines are indented. This is called the reverse indentation or hanging indent method.
- Use a long dash to indicate that an author's entry name is repeated.
- All entries on this page should have a corresponding parenthetical documentation in the paper's body.
- To avoid plagiarism, *all* information gleaned from research sources and borrowed for use require an entry for documentation. If you borrow more than three consecutive words from a source, document the information to credit the source/researcher.

Guiding Questions: These questions will help to organize and to gather facts for the Captured in Stone Project:

1. What is the name of the person you read about?
2. What significant quotes, golden lines, or key passages relate the kind of character your person exhibits? Include the page numbers/source information for these key ideas.
3. In five sentences, summarize the life of your selected person.
4. What qualities of that life qualify him/her to have his/her face on a monument? State the historical, social, philosophical, cultural, or political value of your candidate.
5. In what ways do you relate to your selected person? Do you have similar experiences? The same personality? If you were in the same/similar situation, how would you react? In what ways are you different?
6. Does this person remind you of another famous person, a movie, or a book character?

7. How is this person's life relevant to your life? What about this person's life applies to our day and age? Is there a life message/moral in this person's role modeling?
8. From what three to five books/sources did you gather information about your person?

Audience, Format, and Voice: To give your piece voice and to lend authenticity to the task, adopt the role of a nominator and write as if you will present your research to a selection committee. Your tone will be persuasive as well as informational.

RESOURCE 4.3

Memorializing Virtue—Research Topic

Background: South Dakota is famous for its rugged Black Hills, where soon a second colossal sculpture will memorialize a historically influential figure. Begun in 1948 by sculptor Korczak Ziolkowski, the stone sculpture in progress features the Oglala Lakota warrior Chief Crazy Horse astride a stallion with his arm and pointed hand stretched out over the horse's mane. Being carved out of Thunderhead Mountain on land considered sacred by some Oglala Lakota, the sculpture's final dimensions are planned to be 641 feet wide and 563 feet high. If completed, the monument may be the world's largest sculpture (Buleen, 2020).

Similar desires to memorialize influential figures through sculpture abound. Another such renowned effort surfaces in The Old Hall of the House, now called National Statuary Hall, in Washington, D.C. Each state has two statues; occupying a central viewing room and corridor locations throughout the building, these notable citizens were soldiers, missionaries, statesmen, inventors, or others who contributed something significant to that state's history.

Sometimes this commemoration of influential people comes in other forms. For example, the Heard Museum in Phoenix, Arizona—founded in 1929 by Dwight and Maie Heard—sponsors the annual Spirit of the Heard Award to recognize a living individual who has demonstrated a level of personal excellence in any of the areas that are consistent with the mission of the Heard Museum, which is to educate the public about the heritage and the living cultures and arts of Native peoples. The award is a national award with an emphasis on individuals who are members of a Southwest tribe or community.

As noticed with the Heard example, awards and buildings are often named after people who make significant contributions to society. We saw this happen locally when the Arbor at the Aaniiih Nakoda College campus at Fort Belknap Agency, Montana, was dedicated to Big Sky, Joe Ironman, Sr., in September 2013. The Arbor was named after Ironman, a holy man with the Gros Ventre and Assiniboine tribes of Fort Belknap, because of the sacrifices he made while dedicating his life to the preservation of the philosophy of Indian ancestors. He held on to language, ceremony, Indian philosophy, and Indian ways, preserving them for future generations. For these contributions and for his generous spirit and support of education, we honor and remember him today.

Topic: Throughout history, various people have influenced our world, exerting effort and making sacrifices to improve social, political, and economic conditions. Think about a person in history you know or have studied and consider that individual's importance/impact. Write a research report in which you demonstrate that person's importance/impact on today's world. Discuss the sacrifices this person exerted and assess the importance and/or impact of those efforts that make the person eligible for commemoration.

Whether you think as large as the Crazy Horse memorial and capturing someone in stone, of a smaller sculpture to commemorate someone's heroism, of a recipient for an award like Spirit of the Heard, or of someone after whom a building or a room might be named,

- Begin by making a list of what constitutes "greatness." What criteria does someone need to meet to qualify for such an award or memorial?
- Next, list as many possible candidates for your chosen award/memorial as you can in one minute. Once you have a series of ideas, select one as your topic.
- After choosing your topic, brainstorm how the candidate matches or embodies the criteria you established.
- Then, gather resources to provide evidence, examples, and illustrations verifying what that person has done to merit the honor a memorial/award will bestow.

Select ONE of the Possible Approaches:

1. If some benefactor were ever to fund a project similar to the Crazy Horse memorial, whose likeness would merit the time enduring honor of being captured in stone? Deliberate and establish a set of criteria you will use in determining probable candidates, then measure your choices against this

list of created requirements. Use research to validate your final selection and write persuasively to convince the audience of the appropriateness of your contestant's virtues.
2. Consider the commemoration efforts of Statuary Hall. Who represents your home state? Who were they and why are they important? What do these people represent or say about their state? Do these persons adequately capture the state's identity? If we were to select additional/different persons to capture the state today, who might those people be? What have they done that makes them worthy? Use research to validate your final selection(s). Write persuasively to convince the audience of the appropriateness of your contestant's virtues.
3. Design an award modeled after the Spirit of the Heard Award. What are the criteria? Why is such an award important or needed? Who might win such an award? What qualifies the person for this accolade? Use research to validate your selection and write persuasively to convince the audience of the appropriateness of your contestant's virtues.
4. Still another target for your writing might be the ANC campus. Notice the classroom names in Little River Learning Lodge or White Clay People Hall: Si Si Ya, Bee Gawn Hay, The Boy, Curly Head; or of buildings: Red Whip Recreation Complex. Who were these people? What did they do to earn memorial status? What sacrifices or contributions did they make to American Indian culture? If you were to select an additional/different person to honor sacrifices and cultural contributions, who might that person be? What has this individual done that makes him/her worthy? Use research to validate your final selection. Write persuasively to convince the audience of the appropriateness of your contestant's virtues.

Caution: This project isn't about Mother's Day, so unless your mother is someone like LaDonna Harris or Wilma Mankiller, resist the temptation to nominate your own mother. The person you select as a focus for your research should have historical, social, philosophical, cultural, or political influence. Furthermore, the intent of this project is that the person is more renowned, capturing the essence of a people or a society, not a single family.

Organization: You might consider an introduction that discusses the possibility and significance of another monument like Crazy Horse, a contemporary Statuary Hall, a local Spirit of the Tribe Award, or a building/room name and the challenges you faced in choosing likely nominees. In another paragraph, outline and define the criteria an individual(s) had to meet to qualify for consideration. Who were your finalists and how did you finally name your winner?

In subsequent paragraphs based on research and personal opinion, provide significant evidence of accomplishments and achievements that testify to your personality's qualifications for such a prodigious memorial. Follow with information regarding the historical, social, philosophical, cultural, or political value of such memorials. In your final paragraph, as you restate the candidate's worth, consider how this person's life is relevant to your life and whether there is a life message or moral in this person's role modeling.

Additional Criteria: You must research fairly broadly and extensively about your chosen person's life. If possible, find and read a biography about this person and use this as your primary source. Include at least four other sources—five total—to lend depth to your research and development to your report. These may be internet articles, chapters or passages about your figure from a larger book or anthology, newspaper clippings, or stories told to you by an elder. Also, using MLA style, include a bibliography labeled Works Cited.

Works Cited Page: A Works Cited page is an alphabetical list of all the sources cited in writing your research paper. Prepare this page using the following tips:

- The Works Cited page is numbered and is always the last page of your paper.
- Entries are listed under the centered heading Works Cited.
- Entries are listed alphabetically.
- Each new entry begins at the left margin. Additional lines are indented. This is called the reverse indentation method.
- Use a long dash to indicate that an author's entry name is repeated if you use more than one source by the same author.
- All entries on this page should have a corresponding parenthetical documentation in the paper's body.
- To avoid plagiarism, *all* information gleaned from research sources and borrowed for use requires an entry for documentation. If you borrow more than three consecutive words from a source, document the information, crediting the researcher.

Oral Presentation: For your final exam, you will present your research to the class. In the role of nominator, you will not only present your candidate to the class, which will act as the selection committee, but also persuade us of your candidate's eligibility for the established award or chosen commemoration. Introduce yourself and say you are here today to nominate the person you researched for whatever award you have determined the candidate is eligible. Then go on to explain what makes the candidate worthy.

Summarize the life of your selected person and relate the kind of character your person exhibits. Focus on what qualities qualify him/her for commemoration. State the historical, social, philosophical, cultural, or political influence of your candidate.

In your conclusion, restate the candidate's worth, tell how this person's life is relevant to contemporary society, and reveal the message or moral in this person's role modeling.

Chapter Five

The Power of Talk and Dialogic Exchange

One of the most effective yet often underused scaffolds for supporting learning is dialogic exchange. Talking is a powerful tool for reflecting, analyzing text, and producing knowledge. Conversation or directed discussion provides a low-stakes format for students to explore their thinking. Talk can motivate and involve students—all students, especially if this talk occurs first in small groups before whole class discussion ensues. The intimacy of a smaller group builds confidence for students who might not otherwise possess the courage to go public with their ideas. They put their ideas on trial in a less threatening environment.

Dialogic exchange is an open discussion featuring authentic questions and a shared voicing of understandings not dominated by any one speaker. Discussion members build on previous comments and engage in dialogue—offering, defending, and revising positions. This kind of interactive talk combats the monologic model where the teacher does all the work and knows all the answers.

Possibly because of its interactive features, Peterson and Eeds (2007) call dialogue a process of co-producing meaning. Dialogic exchanges of information require personal investment and idea sharing. This opportunity for reflective talk gives students permission to think more deeply and to have opinions. Sharing and thinking aloud encourages students to generate meaning from text, whether that text is written or visual. As important questions surface, students wrestle with what they know or think and construct meaning through connections and applications to previous experience, reading, and data encounters.

Borrowing from Bakhtin's (1981) notion of dialogic interaction as essential to discussion, Applebee et al. (2003) defined three key features associated with performance improvement: authentic questions, open discussion, and uptake. In this final talk move, another group discussion member (often the teacher) "takes up" and builds on a previous comment. To achieve this development, to help with the hard work of teaching critical thinking, educators structure their "curriculum as a conversation" (Applebee, 1996, p. 83).

Applebee found that the most effective curricula were organized around specific topics that unified reading, writing, and discussion that took place over an extended period. Such time and integration permit students to voice their understandings and then to revisit that thinking for possible revision or refinement.

When educators harness the power of talk, recognizing that certain types of talk facilitate learning, they create experiences that are more educationally generous. If the teacher proposes a genuine question or provides a provocative text to initiate the discussion and then fades to the fringes—serving not as the sage but as a facilitator who repeats student responses or thinking when conversation stalls, prompts for extended thinking or elaboration, provides wait time, and referees for turn taking and respect—she can evoke desired features of student talk—essentially guiding it to "accountable" levels (see resource 5.1 at the end of this chapter).

In building these scaffolds, Michaels, O'Connor, and Resnick (2008) encourage "accountability to the community, accountability to knowledge, and accountability to accepted standards of reasoning" (p. 286).

When teachers shift from passive paradigms to these more active ones, they may encounter initial difficulties with student reticence and hesitation to participate, with focus on surface issues and shallow findings, or with talk that contributes little to the learning. Peterson and Eeds (2007) remind us that students' previous experiences have made them believe that truth comes only from others; they are programmed to store and parrot back other people's knowledge. Possibly clueless about the difference between problem solving and problem generation, students learn to view a problem as something that just shows up in a textbook or a classroom. The subliminal message in school has been that ideas come from somewhere else, not from individual thought processes.

Early in the implementation process, these impediments may tempt teachers to return to tradition, where students wait for the teacher to do all the work, while they simply come to class prepared to take notes or put to memory the details the teacher expects them to recall. Under this traditional design, students rarely view themselves as capable of uncovering broader meaning, questioning "truth," or reflecting independently on the intellectual or ethical value of a text or learning experience.

Other challenges may come from the teacher who struggles to relinquish control, who resists the temptation to fill silent time with his/her own thinking, or who fears controversy. However, with dialogue as pedagogy, educators provide opportunities for students to engage in reflective processes that include dialogue, writing, inquiry, and other metacognitive activities. These rich, reflective components build mental muscle and integrate the critical thinking skills essential to raising social consciousness.

As students banter, negotiate, weigh, and consider ideas, they develop an enriched, multifaceted understanding of the concept discussed. A text's potential expands through their critical interpretation, under the scrutiny of shared insight and connections. With this learning model, students take ownership of the knowledge production process.

When teachers invite conversation about tough topics into the classroom, they explore the effects of binary thinking, perform myth-busting, promote social justice, and even teach survival skills. Although embracing dialogue pedagogy and hosting difficult conversations in the classroom has huge payoffs, we may find ourselves on the doorstep of fear: fear of the conflict that often ensues when divergent truths meet.

Parker Palmer (2007) encourages teachers to embrace these fears that put us "on the brink of learning" (p. 40) and suggests we begin to decode our fear by interrogating the notion of conflict: "Academic culture knows only one form of conflict, the win-lose form called competition" (p. 38). Palmer invites an alternative form—"consensual decision making—in which all can win and none need lose, in which 'winning' means emerging from the encounter with a larger sense of self than one brought into it" (p. 39). In Palmer's vision, creative conflict means challenging dominant modes of knowing. Such encounters "enlarge our thinking, our identity, and our lives [p. 40]. . . . If we dare to move through our fear, . . . we might abandon our illusion of control and enter a partnership with the otherness of the world" (p. 57). Provocative texts like those listed in textbox 4.2 and those in this book's appendix lead the way toward stimulating conversations and to developing such partnerships.

Like any other necessary skill, students will need to learn how to conduct these rich and productive conversations. This requires teaching, practice, and modeling. At first, the process may flounder as students remain reticent and play it safe by simply skimming the surface. Because tough topics evoke strong opinions, the spirit of collaboration is tested, and tension often mounts. Consequently, trust and community-building exercises need to occur prior to discussion.

In addition, protocols and rules about respect must be established for conducting difficult conversations, where the goal should always be to learn, not to be right. Although some ideas are better than others, we don't want to silence or devalue voices and perspectives as long as they have something valid to contribute.

When encouraging contentious talk in the classroom, two strategies promote success. The first, the Busy Intersection Method, was discussed in chapter 4. Another strategy, designed by Adams, Bell, and Griffin (1997), is the Action Continuum. It is available online and invites conversants to find their places along a continuum of Actively Participating in oppression or bullying to Initiating Change and advocating prevention.

To use the Continuum, teachers might pose a tough topic to complement the reading of a text, such as: How do you respond when people refer to gender fluid people in derogatory ways, make jokes or generalized statements about gender identity, or perpetuate caricatures about sexual orientation? As the topic varies, these questions might just as easily become: How do you respond when people refer to American Indians in derogatory ways, make jokes or generalized statements about all Native Americans, or perpetuate caricatures? Before conversation begins, group members would locate themselves on the Continuum.

This process allows for a barometer test of the room while also showing the range of reactions to a given topic. Besides indicating where everyone initially stands, the Continuum suggests there is room to move. If taking such a barometer test of the room is not an option, the teacher might present a scenario and react to it personally or by using a fictional person.

During dialogue mediation, teacher feedback reveals appreciation for idea sharing when any suggestions for revision are couched in relationship-building terms. With such an approach, we preserve the self-respect of those making as well as those receiving prejudicial comments. Adopting a no-flaw focus so as to encourage engaged dialogue doesn't mean the teacher hesitates to intervene if a situation calls for intervention. It also helps to have strategies like CEO mentioned in chapter 4 and comfortable phrases ready to challenge miscues, stereotypes, or off-track thinking: Why do you think that? What evidence can you offer? What might be another way to think? This way the teacher can manage the conversation and invite students to imagine another way to see.

Teachers using tough texts for literary discussions or inviting conversation around controversial social topics are less likely to divorce students from learning or to withhold from them the form of intellectual power earlier described by Palmer. A book like *King of the Screwups* by K. L. Going from the list textbox 4.2, for example, opens the classroom to dialogue about bullying, LGBTQ issues, and abusive behaviors. While students will probably not require much prompting with this book, Talking Points (see resource 5.2, which was originally published in *English Journal* in 2012, at the end of this chapter) illustrate how to leverage the text on challenging issues to maximize engagement and to increase student agency. Talking Points for additional titles are available at www.thinkingzone.org.

According to Lee S. Shulman (1997), ". . . scholarship in all of its forms becomes consequential only as it is understood by others—others who are engaged in related processes of discovery, invention, and investigation—and thus it becomes consequential as it stimulates, builds upon, critiques, or otherwise contributes to any community of scholars who depend on one another's discoveries, critical reviews, and inventive applications to move the work of the field ahead" (p. 26). Although Shulman was speaking to/about researchers, his statement endorses the value of talk in any learning community. What are classrooms if not communities of scholars?

Given these multiple advantages, dialogue transforms classrooms into talking zones and promises achievement as well as strides toward social justice. Through talk, we can hopefully reach a level of understanding that unmasks ignorance and dispels fear.

ARGUMENT LITERACY

Teaching students these rules of scholarly conduct also prepares them to write persuasively, to construct an argument. Argument literacy occurs after such training because students learn to listen closely to the viewpoints of others; to summarize them, comparing and contrasting recognizable positions, weighing evidence, or spotting contradictions; and to make their own relevant argument to continue the conversation of ideas. The values, actions, and atmosphere of a school are lived first by students in their conversations.

Using visual or print texts as catalysts for sparking conversations on complex social issues, we raise social consciousness and support collaborative conversation. Students who experience opportunities to openly discuss what's awry about the society in which they live, to read a text as social protest literature, or to develop a body of knowledge about contemporary social conditions and to critically examine the culture that created those conditions develop civic awareness, critical thinking skills, and argument literacy. Images can be used with great success in classrooms. These include satirical cartoons from local newspapers, Banksy's graffiti art, and spoof ads available at Adbusters.org.

Satirical cartoons work effectively to stimulate conversation on relevant social issues because of their currency. For example, in a unit designed for high school Junior English, students might study the techniques for creating satirical humor. After reviewing the figures of speech that sustain satirical writing and startle readers into attention, students not only recognize how these devices demand an exercise of critical intelligence but extend the dimensions of meaning in a work of literature. These multiple encounters with both print and visual text lead to their writing a satire of their own (see resource 5.3 at the end of this chapter).

Satire, a technique that employs wit—either bitter or gentle—to ridicule a subject intrigues young adults because satire often raises questions about current events, political decisions, social institutions, or human behaviors. By provoking thought and focusing attention on foibles, satire seeks to inspire change or reform, or at least to keep other people from falling into similar folly or vice.

Banksy images also engender copious opportunities for critical thinking and readily inspire reflection in young adults. A Google image search for *Banksy* will uncover a plethora of provocative pictures, such as a tiger breaking free of a barcode cage, a painter whitewashing indigenous cave paintings, or his signature rat with a paw dripping paint who has painted the message: "IF GRAFFITI CHANGED ANYTHING, IT WOULD BE ILLEGAL."

Banksy is a pseudonymous England-based graffiti artist, political activist, film director, and painter. Known for his contempt for the government in labeling graffiti as vandalism, Banksy is a controversial figure who inspires admiration and provokes outrage in equal measure. Featured on streets, walls, and bridges of cities throughout the world, his satirical street art and subversive epigrams combine irreverent dark humor to make political and social commentary.

A third source for stimulating conversation, spoof ads are a form of culture jamming, a term coined in 1984. According to the Center for Communication and Civic Engagement (CCCE), culture jamming denotes a tactic used by many anti-consumerist social movements to disrupt or subvert mainstream cultural institutions, including corporate advertising. The CCCE is located in the Department of Communication at the University of Washington and is co-sponsored by the Department of Political Science.

Culture jamming is often seen as a form of *subvertising* (n.d.) with intentions to expose apparently questionable political assumptions behind commercial culture. Common tactics include re-figuring logos, fashion statements, and product images as a means to challenge the idea of "what's cool" along with assumptions about the personal freedoms of consumption. Culture jamming presents a variety of interesting communication strategies that play with the branded images and icons of consumer culture to make consumers aware of surrounding problems and diverse cultural experiences that warrant their attention.

After selecting a provocative image, teachers might create critical thinking conditions with three simple questions: 1) What idea does the image convey? 2) What does it mean? 3) Why does it matter? (Or why doesn't it?). Other conversation starters might include those in textbox 5.1. The idea is to generate thoughts that can then be further examined and interrogated. Following a unit on image analysis with a written analysis (see resource 5.4 at the end of this chapter) reinforces argument literacy.

TEXTBOX 5.1

Examine this image; take sixty seconds of silent thought. Then answer each question.

1. What word(s) or phrase(s) come to mind as you look at this image?
2. Which details of this image capture your attention?
3. What questions does this image prompt you to ask?

With these analysis, argument, and public conversation skills, we give students access to forms of intellectual capital that have power in both the corporate and the academic worlds. These skills also provide access for those wishing to enter political and social conversations as they vie for resources or rally to promote positive change. A thinking, democratic populace should possess the skills necessary for interrogating social and political practices and policies.

For additional critical thinking topics, teachers can monitor current events. For example, the Associated Press circulated a news story in December 2004 about a company offering a way to keep loved ones near. Based in Chicago, LifeGem crafts diamonds from the ashes of cremated loved ones. Reading that story invites students to wonder whether they would consider this form of commemoration for a loved one and to support their choice with reasons.

Similarly, the April 2004 issue of *Reader's Digest* featured an article, "Skin For Sale," which described how Headvertise, a Providence, Rhode Island, firm, targets college students in need of extra spending money who can earn it by slapping temporary tattoo ads on their foreheads. These live billboards earn up to $200 a week. With this topic, students engaged in lively discussion about whether they would consider renting out their faces for such a purpose, pointing out the embarrassment that might arise with a condom advertisement on one's forehead and ranting about the exploitation of companies that target vulnerable populations. Discussions like these lead to the writing of Cultural Critiques (see resource 5.5).

Furthermore, every year, people around the world celebrate Banned Books Week (BBW) by reading, writing about, and presenting a banned or challenged book (see resource 5.6). Typically held during the last week of September, BBW is an annual event celebrating not only the freedom to read but the importance of the First Amendment. It highlights the benefits of free and open access to information while drawing attention to the harms of censorship by spotlighting actual or attempted book bannings across the United States. It also honors the power of literature.

Whether curriculum stops at intellectual understanding of texts or includes an action phase is a question for local contexts to resolve. A curriculum that includes such topics aims at helping students recognize the discrepancy between ideals and the status quo. After multiple opportunities to examine these discrepancies, students come to realize that what they hear doesn't have to be what they believe. Curriculums so designed invite students to decide for themselves what action, if any, is appropriate to take in closing the discrepancy gap.

As students engage in dialogue and co-produce meaning, they learn that critical thinking comes only after they move beyond the tenacity of individual will, beyond influences from family, church, peer group, social convention, or law, and beyond justification toward a pre-determined outcome. Not rooted in mere feeling or long-held opinion, critical thinking requires actually having evidence to substantiate belief.

Learning to think critically requires considerable teacher facilitation because students will resist the discomfort of uncertainty. A feeling of being lost or confused accompanies this productive learning, and learners who are disinclined to endure disorientation will require help to manage the learning wobble and to reach a level of more scientific reasoning. Because we don't welcome the feeling of inadequacy that doubt brings, we may grab onto the first viable explanation or solution to stop the discomfort engendered by doubt.

Even though doubt triggers the desire to discover, it can also cause a premature shutdown of the inquiry process. Until students learn to welcome confusion as part of the learning process and until they grow confident in the stages of critical thinking, they will require nurturing and frequent reminders to withhold forming an opinion until after they have examined the evidence.

RESOURCE 5.1: TEACHER PROMPTS TO SUPPORT STUDENT TALK

- "Read these six leads and tell me which you like best and why."
- "What makes a good article? What else? Can anyone add on to that?"
- "You mention key elements; what are those key elements?"
- "What about the sentence structure makes it effective? How is the sentence constructed?"
- "What are some similarities you see? Name them."
- "It's entertaining—how?"
- "Because why? Why do you say that?"
- "How do you feel about that?"
- "Those are some strong words; what evidence can you offer?"
- "Who can put into their own words what Sally Sue just siad?"

RESOURCE 5.2

Talking Points for *King of the Screwups*

1. So often we remain silent about the issues that really matter; we don't say the things that need to be said. Instead, we tell social lies, either saying what we don't mean or lying by omission. Going reveals this issue multiple times in her book:

    > "I'm sure you don't want to go to a museum on your first day here," Aunt Pete says, turning to me. It's somewhere between a question and a statement, and once again I can't tell which answer he wants. The honest answer is definitely no.
    >
    > "We could, uh, go to the museum," I say. "I like museums. . ." (p. 41)
    >
    > Is there anything else you want to say?
    >
    > There is. I want to say thanks for taking me in, and thanks for going running, and maybe tell him that I don't really care what he wears because I've seen men in just about everything you can imagine on the runway, but instead I say this:
    >
    > "Just that you're not my father," (p. 67)

    Reading Judith Viorst's lively essay "The Truth about Lying" can stimulate further talk on this topic.

2. To what degree is Liam's drunkenness, casual sex, detentions, defiance, and other delinquent behavior a cry for his father's attention? An escape from verbal and emotional abuse? "Just being a teenager"?
3. Perhaps you have paled beside someone who stands in the limelight: a modeling mother at whom others don't just look; their eyes linger, or a business man-of-the-year father. How does it feel to be in the shadows when others receive awards and attention? Why don't we celebrate another's success more enthusiastically?
4. When he realizes Liam is a fashion Einstein with an eye for color, a knack for sales, and a flair for style, Eddie asks: "Are you gay? . . . I know it's a stereotype, but I had to know. . . . And sometimes stereotypes can be accurate" (p. 120). Under what circumstances are stereotypes accurate? What about dangerous? What does (or might) it feel like to be a victim of stereotyping? How might stereotyping be a form of bullying?
5. Reread pages 132–33 and consider the teens' treatment of Darleen. To what degree is she stereotyped? Why do people judge her? Why do people respond so harshly to different ideas and behaviors? What about social activism scares us?
6. What is your response to people like Allan Geller, so motivated by arrogance and jealousy that they would deprive another person of success, that they treat everyone else like lesser beings and are unable to express pride for another's achievement?
7. On page 134, as Liam's dad accuses, does our culture place "far too much value on sports"? Is having a good body more important than talent? Why should/shouldn't the arts be short changed for a basketball team?
8. Liam asks his uncle why he dresses in women's clothes and wears makeup in his glam-rock shows:

> "Art, glamour, theater. . . . It's not so different from modeling, really. You get onstage and strike a pose. Plus, I feel good when I dress up, and men don't usually get to experience that. But why shouldn't we?"
>
> "Doesn't it bother you that people don't get it?"
>
> "Nope," he says. "If you know what you love, it doesn't matter what other people think. Besides, people are challenged when they're uncomfortable. Glam stretches the boundaries. Gender boundaries, fashion boundaries . . . Glam, punk, rap, metal—they all make people stop and stare. It's good for 'em." (pp. 179–80)

When have you been misunderstood for a behavior, a preference, a mode of dressing? What is something you've done to push the boundaries? Did people understand your motives?

9. Discuss Pete's line about getting on stage and striking a pose and later Liam's line that "fashion's all about fantasy. . . [and] escaping reality" (p. 198); how might these be metaphors for life? To what degree do we seek to "[glitz] up something common" (p. 150) or "[add] something flashy to something ordinary" (p. 150)?
10. Consider Darleen's advice at the novel's conclusion. Why do we believe someone else's assessment that we're "popular and shallow and stupid" instead of seeing our positive side, being "brave and talented and funny" (p. 294)? Why do we "judge on the surface, without getting to know what's underneath" (p. 293)? Why do we care so much about what others think instead of caring more about what we think of ourselves?

RESOURCE 5.3

Writing Satire

Recall the various pieces of satire we have read in this unit and try your hand at this art form. Consider modeling your satire after the style of one of the great writers featured in this unit or invent your own mockery of human foibles. Consider some aspect of life, society, or humanity where you see room for reform. Look back at your Writer's Notebook, at the entries where you listed your pet peeves, discussed what "grinds your gears" or annoys you, talked about traditions that might require altering, and outlined what you are tired of hearing about. Choose one of these topics and explore it in satirical style.

1. For example, you could, as Mark Twain did in "A Fable," write a fable in which you use animal characters to make a point about human nature. Like Twain, you might even start your fable with "Once upon a time. . . ." To begin the process, choose two opposite human qualities, like pomposity and gullibility or wisdom and foolishness, then brainstorm an animal that can represent these qualities. Place your animal characters in a modern setting to make the story relevant, create a good plot with a problem and a resolution, include dialogue, borrow from the techniques of satire (like hyperbole, irony, sarcasm, oxymoron, etc.), and conclude with a moral—this may be an implied or a directly stated moral.
2. Write a character study in poem (like Edwin Arlington Robinson did with "Miniver Cheevy" and "Richard Cory") or paragraph form in which an ironic "surprise" ending throws new light on the character you are describing. For example, you might write about a person who seems popular but

who is actually quite lonely, or about someone who seems kind but in the end proves false and calculating. The irony may be situational or dramatic.
3. Choose a folly or an error of the world and present it for inspection in a way that allows us to laugh at the foible and hopefully seek to correct it. You may use gentle humor—poking good-natured fun at the problem—or you may attack a serious evil by showing the excesses and imbalances of human nature.
4. Write an essay in which the chief effect you intend (beauty, sordidness, strength, weakness, etc.) is combined with elements of its opposite. Or think of some vices that are encouraged by our "heroism" and some virtues that result from our "crimes."
5. Write convincingly about an issue or concern you see in the culture around you. Some possible popular topics include

   - To Read This Essay, Press One
   - Television's Power to Provide Front-Row Seats to Global Suffering
   - Politically Correct Free Speech
   - Would You Like Fries With That?: Serving Up Obesity in America
   - Youth Culture for Sale
   - You Can't Eat Ice Cream with Sprinkles and Wear a T-Shirt with the Slogan *The World Sucks*

6. Select one of your pet peeves and turn your dislike for any human foible/habit into an exaggerated story about why the behavior bugs you so.

RESOURCE 5.4

Analysis of a Visual Argument

Visual arguments are ubiquitous, instantaneous, and powerful. They impact us in less time than it takes to read this sentence. Visual arguments are also economical, since it can take pages of words to unravel the meanings of one photograph or image that a picture can impart efficiently. Out of the thousands of messages that bombard us on a daily basis—from billboards to print sources to television to radio to the Internet—those visual arguments that grab our attention help us identify our dominant socio-personal-political concerns. Awareness of the images that most affect us also helps us determine whether we wish to resist, embrace, or re-create these images and what they represent.

1. Isolate a visual image that has grabbed your attention for whatever reason(s).

2. Although you will write for varying audiences this semester, consider the audience for this assignment to be the members of our class. The Visual Argument can be a photograph, the visual component of an ad, an image of a painting, a CD cover, a cartoon, an article of clothing, product packaging, architecture, a tool, or anything else visual that seems to make a strong point or suggest a significant stance on something by virtue of its appearance—layout, design, color, shape, composition, texture, etc.—rather than by virtue of words. If an ad contains a lot of words, make sure you focus on the visual elements rather than on the verbal context.
3. Next, write two or three substantial paragraphs (400–500 words) in which you state the image's stance/message/thesis/argument (this must be a complete sentence, not just a phrase stating the topic—in essence (not necessarily repeating these words verbatim), complete the following: More than anything else, the creator(s) of this image want(s) me to accept or believe that . . .
4. Describe the intended audience as you perceive it (include some discussion of major values held by the audience that the creator[s] of the image are probably counting on).
5. Describe the strategies being used to convey this stance.
6. Evaluate these strategies' effectiveness (and/or ineffectiveness) in relation to the argument or message and the target audience.
7. Include an MLA-style Works Cited entry at the end of your comments.
8. Be prepared to share your analysis with the class orally, not as a formal speech but more as a share and explain session.

RESOURCE 5.5

Cultural Critiques

For this essay (3+ pages with citations/research) you will write a critique. The critique features a more restrained tone than the rant, but just as explicitly defines its position. Like rants, critiques use voice, story, context, and vivid details to paint a picture of the argument the writer is making.

With a critique, you are making an evaluative or ethical argument about some topic, event, or cause that you care deeply about. Your critique's tone can be serious, funny, or something in between.

Begin by looking critically at the signs of popular culture—such as fashion trends, consumer products, technological innovations, television programming, or media blitzing. From these pervasive messages, we can read and translate the often invisible ideological views that shape our society. In much the same way that we'd analyze more traditional academic texts, we can analyze cultural practices, developments, and objects.

The ultimate goal of this writing invitation is to consider a cultural practice, development, or object and to explain what it reveals about our culture/society.

- Cultural *practices* are the ways people do particular things (such as celebrating holidays) in a given culture.
- Cultural *developments* are changes or trends that occur in a culture. Examples of cultural developments might be the fact that people are reading more electronic texts or participating in social networking.
- Cultural *objects* are single objects that are a part of larger practices or developments (such as Kindles, Droid smart phones, or jeggings).

Semiotics is the study of signs—not just literal signs like billboards and traffic lights but less concrete signs like facial expressions, too. Do you ever make assumptions about people based on how they choose to look? Whether conscious or not, how we "make ourselves up," how we "package the product" is another sign. We read a young man with dreadlocks, one with a buzz cut, and one in a mohawk differently because each sends a message, a sign.

Because consumer culture plays such a huge role in our lives, we are wise to analyze the artifacts of mass production as signs of larger cultural values or beliefs. Even seemingly neutral objects carry meaning beyond their obvious uses. Consider a traditional public school student desk, for example, and read the desk as a sign:

Step #1: Consider its context.

- With what things can this object be associated? (Potential answers: classrooms, schools, learning, students, and teachers)
- Of what system(s) is it a part? (Potential answers: public schooling, theater)
- How is it different than other models/types/styles? (Potential answers: chair attached, wood and metal versus plastic, uncomfortable, restricts movement, oppressive, gives a sense of safety)
- Is it part of a pattern? Are there other things like it? (Potential answers: Other things in school systems that are restrictive are bells, hall passes, hand raising, rules, dress codes, closed campus, security cameras, and visitor management systems)

Step #2: Ask why.

- Why is this object structured/used/built/designed as it is? (Potential answers: Uncomfortable design deters students from falling asleep or day dreaming, easily moved or arranged into rows)

Step #3: Reflect on this sign's significance.

- What does this object reveal about our cultural ideology, values, beliefs, fears, desires, wishes, regrets, accomplishments, etc.? (Potential answers: Ability to exert control, sends a message of conformity and uniformity, what works for one may not work for all—not all body sizes fit in the "one size fits most" design)

This exercise illustrates the value of semiotics. It demonstrates the necessity of analyzing cultural objects and trends to get at the larger, more meaningful ideological implications inherent within them. Cultural criticism also encourages us to look for patterns in trends or behavior and then to consider these details together to make a broader claim about the larger implications of these details.

With this writing invitation, one writer opened his essay by asking: "If you are living in the heartland of suburbia, where the biggest 'off-road obstacle' you are going to encounter is the speed bump at the entrance of Starbucks, do you need to drive a Hummer?" He went on to analyze the details of this SUV's construction which make it possible for the wealthy not only to communicate their power and influence but to lord them over the have-nots.

Another writer selected military trends in female fashion and claimed that they reflect women's anxiety about current economic woes and women's desire to send a message about being strong, bold, courageous, capable, and persistent—much like Rosie the Riveter, the cultural icon of the 1940s.

Once you've decided upon the focus for your critique, collect evidence and make a claim about its significance. Like a semiotician might, think critically about your chosen practice, development, or object and analyze it. Cultural forms reflect life, culture, and societal issues just as literature does, and they can be as readily analyzed for their meaning. Adding references from other sources lends credibility and authority to your voice, strengthening your argument.

RESOURCE 5.6

Celebrating Your Right to Read

> "It's not just the books under fire now that worry me.
> It is the books that will never be written.
> The books that will never be read. And all due to the fear of censorship.
> As always, young readers will be the real losers."
> —Judy Blume (n.d.)

Background: According to the American Library Association (ALA), "Banned Books Week emphasizes the freedom to choose or the freedom to express one's opinion even if that opinion might be considered unorthodox or unpopular and stresses the importance of ensuring the availability of those unorthodox or unpopular viewpoints to all who wish to read them." In 2008, the ALA designated September 27–October 4 as Banned Books Week. Posters advertising the event feature a collage theme celebrating three frequently challenged authors: Laura Ingalls Wilder, Judy Blume, and Stephen King. The year's slogan proclaims: "Closing books shuts out ideas, closes possibilities, and limits understanding." Check out www.ala.org/bbooks for more information on the event and its purposes.

A challenge is an attempt to remove or restrict materials, based upon the objections of a person or group. A banning is the removal of those materials. Challenges do not simply involve a person expressing a point of view; rather, they are an attempt to remove material from the curriculum or library, thereby restricting the access of others. The positive message of Banned Books Week: Free People Read Freely is that due to the commitment of librarians, teachers, parents, students, and other concerned citizens, most challenges are unsuccessful and most materials are retained in the school curriculum or library collection.

Books are usually challenged with the best intentions—to protect others, frequently children, from difficult ideas and information. However, these challenges are acts of censorship and limit intellectual freedom, topics about which many have passionate opinions. For example, according to Supreme Court Justice William O. Douglas (1953): "Restriction of free thought and free speech is the most dangerous of all subversions. It is the one un-American act that could most easily defeat us" (p. 20).

Topic: Select and read two to three frequently challenged books; choose classics or books that might be likely to also appear on the Advanced Placement (AP) Exam. See the suggested list or check with me if you are unsure about a book's suitability, since I want this assignment to serve you in multiple ways. I also want you to read at least two reviews of the book(s) you ultimately choose for your paper. To provide a starting point for literary criticism, check out www.ipl.org.

Other credible sources to consult include *Children's Literature in Education, English Journal, The ALAN Review, The Journal of Adult and Adolescent Literacy, Booklist Magazine, American Libraries, Signal Journal,* and *The Horn Book Magazine.*

**NOTE: Teachers will want to update this writing invitation to reflect developmentally appropriate practice and the teaching context. This task was prepared in 2008 for AP students.

Organization: You might wish to begin your paper with information about the practice of censorship through book banning. You might do this with a quote, an anecdote about personal experience with censorship, or even a startling scenario, warning about the effects of censorship. Perhaps follow with how you feel about book banning, supporting your own opinion with that of authorities on the subject.

Then, in your thesis tell which book(s) you read, identifying for what reasons they are frequently challenged and whether you deem them worthy of that status. In the body, discuss the areas of the book you feel may create dissonance for some readers, quoting passages to illustrate. In addition, to explore merits of the book, quote especially valuable passages, where life lessons, redeemable qualities, or reasons to read the book occur.

Next, report what scholars and critics have to say about the merits or shortcomings of your book(s). Finally, close with your position on the subject of banned books in general and of these books in particular. Based on this collected, balanced evidence, does the book deserve to be banned? Is it worthy of its objectionable status? Would you recommend this book to anyone? Why or why not?

Additional Criteria: Include a Works Cited page with this paper. We will review the style rules and guidelines for this process. Suggested Titles: (Available on the classroom shelves and likely to appear on the AP exam)

* indicates one of the 100 Most Frequently Challenged Books

Books Challenged/Banned for Social Reasons

*Annie on My Mind, Nancy Garden
**The Catcher in the Rye*, J. D. Salinger
**The Chocolate War*, Robert Cormier
*The Color Purple, Alice Walker
*Brave New World, Aldous Huxley
**Lord of the Flies*, William Golding
*Of Mice and Men, John Steinbeck
One Flew Over the Cuckoo's Nest, Ken Kesey
The Scarlet Letter, Nathaniel Hawthorne
**Killing Mr. Griffin*, Lois Duncan
*Ordinary People, Judith Guest
**Flowers for Algernon*, Daniel Keyes
Fools Crow, James Welch

Books Challenged/Banned for Political Reasons

Animal Farm, George Orwell
1984, George Orwell
Bury My Heart at Wounded Knee, Dee Brown
The Jungle, Upton Sinclair
**Slaughterhouse Five*, Kurt Vonnegut
Uncle Tom's Cabin, Harriet Beecher Stowe

Books Challenged/Banned for Religious Reasons

Dragonwings, Laurence Yep
Frankenstein, Mary Shelley
**The Giver*, Lois Lowry
**Bridge to Terabithia*, Katherine Patterson
The Golden Compass, Phillip Pullman

Books Challenged/Banned for Being Obscene

**Forever*, Judy Blume
**The Handmaid's Tale*, Margaret Atwood
Madame Bovary, Gustave Flaubert
Winter in the Blood, James Welch

Other Challenged/Banned Books

Whale Talk, Chris Crutcher
**I Know Why the Caged Bird Sings*, Maya Angelou
**Song of Solomon*, Toni Morrison
**The Pigman*, Paul Zindel
Snow Falling on Cedars, David Guterson
Fallen Angels, Walter Dean Myers

Chapter Six

Reading Cultural Identity Literature

When headline news carries reports about racially motivated food fights at high schools where police have to be called in to subdue students with chemical spray, worry likely fills the minds of teachers across the country who strive to provide safe and secure environments for students. Some probably also wonder what more educators might do as bridge builders or liaisons to allay such tensions.

The Latin word for "bridge builder" is *pontifex*, a title originally used for a certain group of priests in ancient Rome who served as scholars, liaisons, and disciples or teachers (Miller, 2014). To make philosophy and theological principles more relevant to everyday life, the pontifex told parables or stories.

Not only a tool for teaching, story is a means of connection. When we hear people's stories, when we share intimate aspects of self and tribe and culture, when we accept new ways of knowing, we pierce the balloons of old thought to allow prejudice to dissipate. Until we hear such stories, it often doesn't occur to us that others have a story of their own, that they are anything but the thieves or losers or infidels that we perceive them to be. Hearing another's story has the potential to deflate our self-importance, making room for other perspectives. As a result of this potential, story serves as a pontifex.

Educators play a role in this bridge building, in part, by infusing the curriculum with rich connections to students' cultural and linguistic backgrounds. Cultural Identity Literature (CIL) is one vehicle for providing that connection.

The term CIL serves to enlarge the traditional term *multicultural literature* (MCL) because many people who use the term MCL use it to identify literature that is diverse in geography, race, or ethnicity. While there is no single definition of the term "multicultural literature" as it is applied to books for children and young adults, Gopalakrishnan's (2011) speaks powerfully to the purpose of multicultural literature: to validate "the sociocultural experiences of previously underrepresented groups, including those occurring because of differences in language, race, gender, class, ethnicity, identity, and sexual orientation" (p. 5).

Although social scientists don't agree on any one definition of culture, many of those who study culture (Gay, 2000; Gaitan, 2006; Banks, 2010; Erickson, 2010) identify determinants of culture similar to those named by Gopalakrishnan. When selecting literature for potential course reading lists, an educator might use the acronym GREEN APPLE to remind him or her of eleven common determinants of cultural identity. From the acronym, we can easily produce the list: gender identity, religion, ethnicity and race, economic class/socioeconomic status, name/family, age, place (national territory/geography), perception of belonging, language, and exceptionality—whether gifted or challenged.

Those eleven factors determine our way of thinking, feeling, believing, and behaving. As cultural markers, these aspects shape one's identity, and literature studies embrace greater diversity when they represent each one.

Cultural Identity Literature is that which targets one or more of these eleven identity determinants so as to promote self-understanding or to enlarge one's perspectives of diverse cultures and identities. A study from Germany published in 2017 (Böckler et al.) suggests that understanding the self leads to an increased ability to understand the thoughts and feelings of others. Psychologists consider this empathizing or perspective-taking process to be a crucial socio-cognitive skill. It is a skill required not only in everyday life, but also with regard to cross-cultural comprehension.

To the extent that literature might influence this understanding, reading CIL is one form of targeted training for building self-understanding and for imagining the experiences of others. The list of CIL titles in this book's appendix reflects materials that foster not only positive student self-images but assist in developing what Stanbrough, García, and King (2020) identify as "attitudes grounded in respect for and understanding of the diverse cultures of American society" (n.p.).

This attitude development is an issue of priority, according to the National Council of Teachers of English (NCTE). In their Position Statement on Indigenous Peoples and People of Color (IPOC) in English and Language Arts Materials, NCTE calls for such materials. Because of its unique focus, CIL meets this call.

One responsibility of the classroom teacher is to address issues of identity formation. Whether an educator does that in language arts by reading CIL, in social studies by making connections to students' cultural backgrounds as well as enriching their perspectives of diverse cultures, or in health and physical education class by discussing gender and sexuality issues, educators build a sense of belonging and foster intellectual growth.

In the United States where sex is recognized as a socially taboo topic for many people, sex education in the schools is immediately suspect. Yet, denying that aspect of one's identity is like disregarding an element of one's culture. Looking at the topic from another angle, if we were to ask kindergarteners whether they have ever been in love, we would learn that they are ready for honest conversations about love and relationships—the foundation for sexuality education.

Sex ed is not just about reproduction and contraceptive options. It's about self-image, gender stereotypes, and sexual orientation. It's also about communication and power—about expressing one's identity, one's wishes, and one's boundaries. Teachers typically want their students to develop the assertiveness to express themselves so that they are never victims of unwanted intimacy. By encouraging respect and by helping students develop healthy attitudes about their bodies and themselves, we also protect them against sexual coercion, intimidation, and abuse. Shaping attitudes early will hopefully reduce some of the cruelty and bullying that society currently sees with sexting and social media.

Because sexual development is a normal process that all young people experience, they should have access to candid, trustworthy information. If we hope that kindergarteners will grow into secure young adults, then we owe it to them to teach them the developmentally appropriate topics related to sexuality education. Responsibility and respect are the foundation of health—both social and biological.

Whenever a potentially difficult, sensitive, or controversial issue like sex needs to be addressed, a book will likely help a teacher start the conversation. In addition to all of their other purposes, stories are powerful tools for empathy building. It is not a teacher's place to judge another, and teachers usually want their students to understand that personal and family differences should be respected. To do this work with elementary students, a teacher may select the award-winning picture book *And Tango Makes Three* by Justin Richardson and Peter Parnell (2005).

Before teachers use materials that may engender controversy, they should develop context awareness and have a clear rationale with solid objectives as well as alternate selections available. Because the penguin parents in the Richardson/Parnell book are of the same sex, some people might object to children reading/hearing this story. Sending letters home to alert parents and to communicate instructional objectives is an important step. Respecting dissenting opinions is also imperative, which is why alternative selections play an essential part of a well-written rationale (see resource 6.1).

The Richardson/Parnell book is based on the true story of Roy and Silo, two male Chinstrap Penguins in New York's Central Park Zoo, who for six years formed a couple. The book follows a time in the penguins' lives after the pair was observed trying to hatch a rock that resembled an egg. When zookeepers realized that Roy and Silo were both male, it occurred to them to give the penguin pair an egg to hatch. A second egg was obtained from a male-female penguin couple that had previously been unable to successfully hatch two eggs at once. As a family, Roy and Silo hatched and raised the healthy young chick, a female named "Tango" by keepers. As much as the book exposes young readers to the notion of same-sex parent families, it defines love.

For teachers who fear censorship when dealing with critically important but controversial social topics, a rationale is perhaps the most important offensive strategy available. Initially, a rationale provides the vehicle for deep thought on objectives and justification for a book's purpose and value. After this pedagogical reflection and research, rationales tell the principal, superintendent, parents, community, and students why the curriculum includes a certain text or ideology.

A well-written rationale has potential to convince these audiences—these stakeholders—that a text meets essential understandings and learning objectives. Resource 6.1 at the end of this chapter provides a rationale model for the Richardson/Parnell book. With their theory, scholarly research, and sociocultural justifications, rationales answer the following questions:

- What are you planning to teach or trying to accomplish?
- Why are you planning to teach this lesson/unit or trying to accomplish these objectives?
- What content standard or issue does this lesson/unit address?
- What content benchmark does this lesson/unit address?
- What cultural or social need does this lesson/unit address?
- What developmental/personality issue does this lesson/unit address?

A rationale ties research, scholarship, theory, and common-sense knowledge to the decisions we make about teaching; therefore, rationales are an important part of any lesson or unit. A thoroughly written rationale often has seven parts or sections: title, author, awards/critical acclaim, objectives (pedagogical and philosophical explanations/connections), plot description, strategies for addressing sensitive issues, and alternate selections.

Whenever dealing with sensitive issues, teachers do well to remember the need to consider important steps:

1. Always ask—how might an encounter with this topic feel?
2. Craft lesson activities with great care.
3. Build context for the controversial issues and sensitive subjects; front load, prepare.
4. Be certain not to trivialize the experiences of the disempowered or marginalized.
5. Provide ample opportunity for reading and writing, processing and debriefing.
6. Design a safety net; what will you do if emotions take over?
7. Empower students at every turn.
8. Foster a community of learners.
9. Know your district's policy for challenging books/school materials.

Other resources for avoiding censorship as an issue in schools and about writing rationales are available from the National Council of Teachers of English:

- www.ncte.org/about/issues/censorship

A rationale makes visible to all stakeholders a teacher's intention for using particular curricular materials.

Cultural Identity Literature (CIL) like the Richardson/Parnell book can support unity by dispelling some of the myths and misperceptions about diverse lifestyles and cultures. After all, truth doesn't stop being true because we believe something different. CIL also addresses issues of power and oppression and provides an opportunity to view these issues from a different perspective, thereby inspiring empathy building. The force of such literature is in its ability to engage the reader and to break through barriers.

After all, violence often traces back to fear, and knowledge provides an antidote to fear. If we can identify the sound in the dark, our insecurity generally dissipates. Well-crafted cultural identity stories can—for example—draw distinctions, reveal alternate perspectives, and flesh out reality. These stories encourage us to ask hard questions and to constantly interrogate and critique what we do and why certain social practices and beliefs remain in place.

Targeted for youth from the middle grades through high school and early college, CIL books like those annotated and listed in this text's appendix can help youth of all identities to understand their own culture and that of others. This list is not meant to be exhaustive nor exclusive but simply a means of sharing a number of texts that have been tested in classrooms. Reading such texts contributes to the humanizing practice of seeking to sustain more equitable and just practices within and across classroom and school contexts.

These titles provide strong positive images to recall when young people inevitably encounter negative ones. Adolescents often connect with this CIL because they identify with the young adult characters who live lives parallel to their own and who struggle with similar conflicts and issues. The topics of these books are likely to reflect the diverse realties that young people face. One of those realities is difference.

Countless studies reveal the marginalization and harassment faced by students who are different, who do not fit mainstream definitions. This alienation may arise from varied families, distinct economic circumstances, diverse ethnicities, unfamiliar experiences, home settings, religions, and alternate lifestyles. Living on the social margins presents difficult challenges for youth. The alienation that some young people experience as a result of their differences can be alleviated by books that communicate they are not alone in the world.

Reflective of our ever-growing diverse society, young adult literature includes a growing body of work that represents different ethnic and cultural groups. Providing access to these texts potentially increases understanding of self and others because CIL can stretch our vision of ourselves and our world. A democratic English Language Arts curriculum attempts to reflect the experiences and histories of all students, including those representing a range of ethnic and cultural identities.

Offering CIL is one way to address the issues of identity formation, reading motivation, and literacy development for today's youth. With studies of CIL, educators ultimately promote and honor cultural identity. When readers see themselves represented in stories, they realize that they matter, that their experiences count. According to Metzger, Box, and Blasingame (2013), "implementing curriculum of this kind is essential to establishing and maintaining equity in our society" (p. 58). Cultural relevance also plays a role in motivation to read. Because young adult literature has relevance, it communicates to readers in ways that the classics cannot. We foster literary literacy when we present students with engaging reading material that rewards meaningful analysis, demonstrates important connections with their lives, and legitimizes their voices.

Young adult books provide the opportunity to read, to write, and to argue about important issues in a modern context. We don't just want students to read novels; we want to expose them to multiple perspectives, to situations that encourage a critical stance so as to inspire wisdom that might lead to an improved way of living in the world.

USING GREEN APPLE QUESTIONS AS A GUIDE

Literacy sponsorship continues with bridge building, a process facilitated by using Cultural Identity Literature guided by GREEN APPLE questions. Gender identity, religion, ethnicity and race, economic class/socioeconomic status, name/family, age, place (national territory/geography), perception of belonging, language, and exceptionality—whether gifted or challenged—all shape our cultural identities and will affect how we read the word and our world, how we respond to others, and how we live our lives.

Reading with these aspects in mind focuses one's thinking and might stimulate questions that enable us to see more clearly and completely because they multiply our perspectives. Generically, the acronym generates the following questions to guide reading, but these questions are subject to change as the acronym is applied to a specific book or behavior:

Gender Identity: How does gender identity contribute to the novel? What gender boundaries, if any, limit character behavior or create conflict? What, if any, gender role expectations do the characters encounter? If gender is a social construct, what other gender definitions exist in the novel? Thinking of gender as falling on a spectrum, what feminine, masculine, or gender-fluid behaviors define the characters?

Religion: Reflect on what you know, have heard, or experienced about church and religion. Explain how your experiences and understandings might compare, contrast, or align with the beliefs exhibited in the characters. Beyond organized religions, look for any rituals and/or ceremonies which have potential to affect or influence mind, body, and spirit.

Ethnicity and Race: Consider how ethnicity shapes one's worldview. What ethnic markers occur in the text—like a reference to ancestry (German, Sioux, etc.)? What purpose do they serve? How do the characters live out the social practices and customs of their ethnic groups? What descriptive details does the author use to indicate the racial identities of the characters? Consider what these details mean and how they do/don't matter. What privileges or challenges, if any, do the characters experience because of their race?

Economic Class:	What details give clues about the socioeconomic class to which each character belongs? What conditions account for the class differences in the lives lived by the characters? How might these features privilege or disadvantage the characters? To what degree, if any, do characters exhibit a sense of entitlement? How do these identities compare or contrast with your own socioeconomic status?
Name/Family:	Often imparting status or clout, names can send signals about who we are and where we come from. Do any of the characters have names that allow people to make quick judgments and assumptions about them? Consider whether character or family names carry expectations, reputations, or unearned privileges. What are the characters' reactions to any nicknames?
Age:	How does age shape and define the behavior that manifests in the characters? What limitations, expectations, or privileges, if any, are imposed by age?
Place:	How do place and location contribute to and shape character behavior? What limitations, conflicts, restrictions, and/or conveniences result because of place? How has place shaped their identities? How do the characters react to society's expectations for integration?
Perception of Belonging:	How do characters perceive of themselves? How do they want others to perceive of them? How are they presenting themselves? What efforts, if any, do characters make to fit in, to find their niche? What difference makes the characters feel the most different? Consider the degree to which the characters find personal acceptance or feel accepted by others. Some people define themselves as athletes, social justice warriors, theater kids, or Victorian novel readers; how do the characters define themselves in the book you are reading? How do you define yourself? On what do you hang your identity? What identity labels, if any, do others thrust on you that you resist?

Language:	Because we each belong to a unique discourse community with its own vernacular, what do you notice in the languages that are spoken by the characters? Look for any culturally relevant idioms. Consider the discourse community to which you belong; what vernacular/language is common to you?
Exceptionality:	Ability falls on a spectrum—from gifted to challenged. These gifts and challenges may be physical or mental. What exceptionalities do you observe in the characters? In what ways do these traits impose limitations or enable access? How do labels like *perfect* or *normal* function in society?

GREEN APPLE is a learning tool, and leading discussion with the help of the acronym encourages cultural border crossing and seeing from multiple perspectives. A GREEN APPLE discussion has potential not only to challenge dominant modes of knowing but to facilitate the process of producing knowledge from facts. Under the influence of the GREEN APPLE questions, teachers can move students to encounter possibilities for seeing differently so that they can further their growth and development.

Because breaking diversity into discrete categories like those represented in the GREEN APPLE acronym might keep students from looking at intersectionalities between categories, they will require teacher support to consider the other categories and to find overlaps and relationships. For example, names are loaded with cultural meaning; sexism, racism, and classism influence how a person perceives another's name, even when just reading it on paper.

Consider how names like Charley, Geraldo, and Shaniqua can be stereotyped. Separating these cultural identity markers simply allows them to be examined. We are never ONE of these elements at a time; we are always a jigsaw puzzle of all of them, although there are times that one element comes forward and takes the lead, depending on the circumstances. A person might flaunt his or her socioeconomic status, for example, when trying to gain membership into a group or community that places value on such status, and most of us have likely used flirtation strategies to establish a connection and to gauge the interest of others in reciprocating that connection.

Breaking diversity down with GREEN APPLE questions sets in motion a form of analysis that requires learners then synthesize. Reassembling the separate parts that were previously analyzed has potential to form new insights. In this process, GREEN APPLE serves as a resource to stimulate thinking.

From thinking prompts and the discussion and reflection that follow, students can form original concepts.

Although other states have adopted similar policies under the Common Core State Standards Initiative, according to the Montana Common Core Standards for English Language Arts and Literacy in History/Social Studies, Science, and Technical Subjects (Montana Office of Public Instruction, 2011), students who are college- and career-ready in reading, writing, speaking, listening, and language not only comprehend as well as critique, they value evidence:

> Students are engaged and open-minded—but discerning—readers and listeners. They work diligently to understand precisely what an author or speaker is saying, but they also question . . . assumptions and premises and assess the veracity of claims and the soundness of reasoning.
>
> Students cite specific evidence when offering an . . . interpretation of a text. They use relevant evidence when supporting their own points in writing and speaking, making their reasoning clear . . . , and they constructively evaluate others' use of evidence. (p. 8)

These descriptions suggest that, under the influence of the literacy standards, students will grow into discerning, open-minded thinkers who employ sound arguments supported with relevant evidence. A democracy requires the kind of civil discourse described in those student portraits, but this growth doesn't occur without careful and intentional cultivation.

To nurture these rules of scholarly conduct, schools need to become Talking Zones rich with student talk, not dominated by teacher talk. Interactive talk, or dialogic exchange, combats the read and regurgitate method and the monologic model where the teacher does all the work and knows all the answers; it replaces the call and response or initiate, respond, evaluate (IRE) models.

Young adults often enjoy conversing about contentious topics, yearning to voice and to defend their views. Teachers can leverage this interest for debating social issues by crafting conditions that enable this talk to happen productively—no easy task because this new learning typically begins with unlearning.

When offering relatable, provocative topics, teachers may confront parochialism from students who measure and judge behavior, believing in a standardized notion of what it means to be normal or socially acceptable. They may see difference as a defect, a burden, or even a danger. Such socially divisive notions require that educators expand psychological schemata for a broader understanding of the term normal, an expansion that depends on doubt management while we do the important work of normalizing difference. Examining a topic with GREEN APPLE questions to guide reading can assist in this clarity of vision.

Because the GREEN APPLE learning tool encourages identity examination, young people are often reassured to discover that they are not alone in the world. A person's conception of what is normal is largely influenced by social conventions and cultural values, by how society and its institutions define "normal." These values, conventions, and institutions shape cognitive development and account for diversity in the definition of normal, a definition that is subject to change with time, place, and individual circumstances.

Because its idiosyncratic meaning exists in the mind of the speaker who is limited by personal experience, normal can be a crazy-making word. For some individuals, living with a neurological condition called synesthesia may be normal, while for others normal speech may involve a challenge like stuttering, or normal may simply mean possessing common sense and manners.

In addition to being influenced by biological and neurological factors, human diversity arises from cultural differences—differences that shape one's identity: gender identity, religion, socioeconomic class, ethnicity and race, name/family, age, place, perception of belonging, language, and exceptionality—whether giftedness or other special needs (GREEN APPLE).

Nevertheless, we toss the word *normal* around as if all people share a common set of experiences, values, or beliefs. In fact, we individually set the bar and define the terms of what normal means when we examine a behavior guided by one of these cultural angles. Under the influence of this social, cultural, and cognitive conditioning, we make pronouncements like: "It's not normal to be that passionate about ballet!" Or, we exclude, insult, or shun someone whom we judge a misfit.

Because the careers of a plethora of professionals—from the mental health and pharmaceutical professions to the advertising industry—are built on the notions of what is "normal" and "abnormal," to hope that the situation can change may seem formidable, but as power shifts and people grow more sensitive to difference and to the harm in binary thinking, society may be ready to rethink those concepts.

WHY CHANGE WILL COME SLOWLY

Educators can foster change by encouraging youth to ask tough questions and to think critically about why society stigmatizes certain differences. An inquiry project will find answers in both psychology and biology. As we combat human psychology and biology, change will come slowly; it will take multiple exposures and a concerted effort on our part to build mental muscle.

To understand how we got to this place where society favors labels and often refers to difference as abnormal, we need to turn to cognitive science for some definitions. Psychologist Jeanne Ellis Ormrod (2008) discusses how children and adults alike often organize information into schemas and scripts as they construct knowledge. A schema is a cognitive framework that helps the brain systematize and make sense of information as we experience the world. For instance, the basic concepts that allow us to quickly identify and classify different types of cookware are schemata.

From these tightly integrated sets of ideas about a specific object or situation, we organize our actions—selecting a cake pan and not a cast iron skillet for baking a birthday cake, for example. As we progress through life, we seek out information that supports this choice while discarding information that disagrees with this behavior. This information contributes to our knowledge structure, and from it we form scripts, the predictable sequence of events related to particular activities, such as a birthday party.

Because of these schemata and scripts, we are conditioned to have certain expectations about how the world works and how certain events should occur. Coloring our view and perspective, these schemata exert a great deal of influence over us and may even hinder us from remembering new information because it does not fit into our cognitive framework.

This compartmentalizing of concepts contributes to cognitive efficiency, allowing us to make an immediate assessment of a situation and to recognize danger, for example. But it may also contribute to cognitive bias. That we prefer one pan over another may be of little consequence in the grand scheme of the universe, but when we use that same schema to exclude an idea entirely—girls don't play with trucks—or to draw conclusions that close off opportunities for understanding the world differently—homosexuality is not normal—prejudice can begin to grow.

Because we humans all have passions, convictions, desires, and predilections, we will exhibit bias. Bias itself isn't a bad thing; it describes our inclination to present or hold opinions based on our experiences and perspectives. The problem occurs when we allow those perspectives to color or discredit valid alternatives. Critical thinking involves a concerted effort to recognize and acknowledge our biases, ultimately taking them into account when weighing evidence and logic so as to ensure that those biases don't unfairly tip the scales in an inappropriate direction.

Furthermore, a willingness to examine our biases is an important step in understanding the roots of stereotypes and prejudice that exist in our society. This is easier said than done, of course, because we have a vested interest in our biases, like religion, and we tend to think that others should believe as we do, that they should share our biases.

Partner these scripts with the psychological need for closure, and we create conditions ripe for closed-mindedness. The human mind has such a strong desire for predictability and a preference for order and structure that we find discomfort in ambiguity. In order to alleviate the distress of the unknown and to regain some measure of sanity, we settle on a decision, even if that decision is not the most accurate or the best answer.

Psychologist Jerome Kagan (1972) claims that this "uncertainty resolution" is a primary determinant of human behavior. When we cannot immediately gratify our desire to know, when we experience the irritation and discomfort of doubt, we become highly motivated to reach a concrete explanation, to return to a state of comfort. This need for closure and this need to end the irritation of doubt lead us to hastily constructed conclusions. These invented explanations or inaccurately drawn conclusions die hard deaths because we are averse to uncertainty and ambiguity and strongly favor predictability.

Besides the effects of psychological conditioning due to schemas and scripts and the human difficulty in managing doubt, our biological preference for symmetry further biases us. The body plans of most animals, including humans, exhibit bilateral symmetry. Symmetry is also prevalent in the physical sciences and is woven into the very laws that govern our universe.

Mario Livio (2005), an astrophysicist at the Space Telescope Science Institute in Baltimore, Maryland, discusses how prizing balance has become a pivotal concept in our ideas about the world, calling symmetry "the paramount tool for bridging the gap between science and art, between psychology and mathematics" (p. 2). He explores our biological preference for symmetry and concludes that it is biasing our perception of the world, influencing what humans find beautiful or even affecting the way we conduct science.

Geoffrey Cowley (1996) also writes about this preference for symmetry, calling it the "beautylust" that programs animals, as well as humans, when looking for certain features in a mate.

Knowing these psychological and biological facts will potentially help us to combat them. Exposure to well-chosen texts can further assist in the process of constructing new knowledge so as to enlarge and revise our schema and scripts. Normalizing the notion of difference, then, will depend not only on managing the frustration that accompanies unknowing but also on building new knowledge as we reach new definitions and awareness.

THE POWER OF QUESTIONING

Developing new schema and scripts will also depend on a willingness to ask questions since asking rich questions contributes to sense making. These questions are more likely to surface when guided by the GREEN APPLE acronym, adding to clarity of vision. Just as readers transform a text as they read, bringing diverse understandings of literary conventions to the reading, these conventions have potential to transform readers, informing them as they respond to textual encounters. If nothing else, a GREEN APPLE reading will reinforce the idea that a text conceivably carries multiple meanings, just as there are many lives in every life.

Asking questions from the angles of gender identity, religion, ethnicity and race, socioeconomic status, name/family, age, place, perception of belonging, language, and exceptionality—whether giftedness or other special needs—provides students with strategies for

- seeing differently and analytically, supplying tools that can help them read various cultural elements
- learning to appreciate the power of multiple perspectives
- enhancing textual reading and building meaning by providing frames in which a variety of interpretations can be articulated
- understanding that meanings are constructed
- encouraging recognition of diversity and respect for difference
- bringing greater visibility to issues of class, language, ethnicity, age, race, geography, religion, exceptionality, and gender that are embedded in texts
- asking big questions (What is happening and how did it get this way? Why do people think that? Is there a better way of knowing/being?)
- exercising a kind of mental flexibility
- revising current ways of knowing
- reading rigorously and seeing more deeply, completely, and intelligently

Using these strategies will not only enable diverse students to tell their stories but will encourage all of us to see beyond ourselves.

In addition, reading guided by the GREEN APPLE acronym has the potential to encourage readers to consider multiple angles, pose unfamiliar questions, devise ingenious solutions, and take interpretive risks. Armed with the skills to deconstruct arguments, readers are better prepared to notice differences, think critically, consider alternate positions, and make more informed, ethical choices. In classrooms that foster dialogic exchange, mutual respect, and an obligation to decency, students might experience a climate where individuals speak from a distinct perspective while remaining open to alternate perspectives.

As explained in chapter 5, dialogic exchange is an open discussion featuring authentic questions and a shared voicing of understandings not dominated by any one speaker. Because dialogic exchanges of information require personal investment and idea sharing, the model gives students permission to think more deeply, to have opinions, and even to be open to revising their opinions.

Sharing and thinking aloud further encourage students to generate meaning from text, whether that text shares the results from a science experiment or a character's behavior. As important questions surface, students grapple with what they know or think and construct meaning through connections and applications to previous experience, reading, and data encounters.

When teachers shift from passive paradigms to more active ones, they may encounter initial difficulties with student reticence and hesitation to participate, with focus on surface issues and shallow findings, or with talk that contributes little to the learning. Chapter 5 discusses some of the reasons for this behavior. However, when we teach young people to evaluate arguments and to make effective arguments of their own, we promote the kind of civil discourse that democracy requires.

As a means to begin opening these pathways to learning, early in the school year a teacher might survey students' thinking by inviting them to write in a ritual called Quickwrite Wednesdays and Think About Thursdays (see resource 3.1 in chapter 3). To do a quickwrite, students write for two to three minutes off a found idea or borrowed line from a text or a short piece of writing, responding to whatever sparks a reaction in the mind of the reader/listener.

On Thursdays, a thought-provoking question or an interesting quote invites thinking. To provide some reflection time, the response period for a Think About is three to five minutes. This rapid response writing process helps writers generate ideas and get words on paper. By writing fast, we hopefully outrun our internal censors and let our own words untangle our thinking.

Teachers should always consider the value of writing along with their students, an action that communicates value in the task. When the writing time has nearly elapsed, the teacher can quietly announce, "Find a way to exit your writing," and the group can then spend five or so minutes sharing their ideas aloud with the entire class or in small groups. As writers read, listeners often notice something striking or effective about another student's writing. We thank any volunteers for sharing and comment specifically on what they have done.

A favored Think About topic for surveying students' triggers comes from Anne Roiphe (1988): "We need to look closely at the border where our empathy ends; there our potential for cruelty begins" (p. 21). Prior to a discussion of what Roiphe may have meant with that proclamation, a person might explore two questions: Where are your borders? On what topics/issues do you experience pangs of intolerance?

During a debrief of this topic, the discussion proctor might encourage those engaged by asking additional questions:

- While you don't have to let go of what you believe or give up your privilege, how might you allow others to be there?
- Is there anything that you might need to unlearn in order to make room for new learning?
- What assumptions do you need to struggle against?
- What steps will you take in these growth processes?

This ritual provides the training grounds for civil discourse because it enables students—especially preservice teachers—to hear diversity of thought and to recognize that their reality, their understanding, their experience is not the only one. It also encourages a deep look within. After all, teaching comes from the core of one's being; it involves our hearts. To examine one's predisposed ideologies, beliefs, and biases is an important step in developing a culturally responsive mindset because our beliefs manifest in our actions. Our beliefs influence our students, our content, our instructional practices, and our way of being in the world.

Therefore, with a topic such as Roiphe's, all students learn to interrogate their biases, to consider alternatives, and to make room for new learning as they struggle against long-held assumptions. They come to realize that what they hear doesn't have to be what they believe. Their beliefs can be informed by facts after considering and accepting experiences that differ from their own. Under the influence of these procedures, reading all texts facilitated by GREEN APPLE questions as a learning tool further builds awareness and encourages empathy building.

To illustrate how the GREEN APPLE questions might work with a text, we can apply it to the book *If I Ever Get Out of Here* by Eric Gansworth (2013). Besides winning a place on YALSA's 2014 list of Best Fiction for Young Adults and being an Honor Recipient of the American Indian Library Association's 2014 Youth Literature Award, Gansworth's book is an honest look at culture, what it means to be marginalized, and how people with vastly different upbringings and identities can clash. It also reveals music's power to tap knowledge, feeling, and insight as well as music's role in catharsis. Allusions to The Beatles abound in the book, with songs and riffs titling every chapter and with considerable history being shared about Paul McCartney's post-Beatles ventures.

That readers don't learn the name of Gansworth's protagonist until page 59 reinforces Lewis Blake's identity crisis and struggle to define himself. Set at the time of the country's bicentennial—a celebration that rubs salt in an old wound on the reservation—the story opens with Lewis submitting to the cutting of his braid, evidence since second grade of his Indianness. Lewis, who lives a complicated and lonely life, wants to be invisible when it suits him—to avoid the stares of store clerks and the whispers about wild or scary Indians from townspeople. Hoping to pass as German, or even Italian, Lewis welcomes this change of identity, thinking that looking more like everyone else might increase his chances at friendship.

As a "brainiac" who can speak his traditional Tuscarora language, Lewis has been tossed into junior high with twenty-two white strangers and struggles to learn their social language and to fit in: "If I could find a good plastic surgeon . . . maybe I could ask for a few modifications, a pull here and there, some skin bleach and suddenly, I wouldn't be that kid from the reservation anymore. I would be like everyone else, a Dear Boy" (p. 31).

Lewis does eventually find friendship with George Haddonfield, a "military base kid" who knows what it means to be on the outside. Despite their remarkable cultural differences, the two boys discover they have a lot in common, including their love for music and The Beatles.

But every time Lewis feels comfortable knowing he has blended in, he experiences the sensation of guilt, "like a garden slug working inside my belly, leaving its slime trail" (p. 49). In his identity struggle, Lewis connects with Paul McCartney. Just as McCartney fought for distinction with Wings and to escape the "Beatle Paul" label, Lewis wants to be Lewis Blake, not Indian Lewis: "I didn't have any objection to being known as an Indian, but couldn't I have my own life as just me? Or like McCartney, was I stuck being expected to play the songs of my first band for the rest of my life?" (p. 159).

Lewis spends the better part of junior high struggling to navigate both the white world and the reservation, wondering whether he can have an identity in both. He doesn't want to choose one to hate and one to love.

Still, at school among white people, Lewis encounters indifferent teachers, isolation, and active violence from Evan Reiniger, a wiry-muscled, wildcat-eyed bully who is impervious to rules and robs Lewis of any safety or security at school. Unable to find an ally, Lewis quits going to school until he accepts that he needs to speak to Evan in his own language, the language of violence.

Focused on the cause of this violence, a college freshman enrolled in a Young Adult Literature course used an adaptation of the Anti-Defamation League's Pyramid of Hate (2005) and applied the graphic to explore how biased behaviors in the treatment of Lewis grow in complexity. One class had discussed the Pyramid while reading Marlene Carvell's *Sweetgrass Basket* and traced the behaviors of Mrs. Dwyer, the headmistress at Carlisle Indian School, as she moves up the Pyramid, seizing every chance to scold and punish, to scorn and criticize, until she commits several acts of bias-motivated violence.

Remembering this progression from Prejudiced Attitudes, to Acts of Prejudice, to Discrimination, and then to Violence, the reader applied these stages to the treatment of Lewis. Her reader response illustrated how Evan Reiniger's acceptance of his dad's stereotyping of Indians as untrustworthy, because a "Teepee Creeper [was] in the sack with his ex" (p. 297), leads to Evan's calling Lewis and Tami "Scummy Welfare Indians" and then to his harassment of Lewis, who endures an act of educational discrimination. In the student's diagram, this hate reaches a pinnacle when Evan physically assaults Lewis.

Another student in the same course developed a word cloud featuring what she considered key elements and themes affecting Lewis. Using the website tagxedo.com, the artist designed a hand-facing palm with words like discrimination, alcoholic, absent father, bullying, and poverty; then, she wrote a brief explanation for her choice: "I see the handprint as being used as a way of saying, 'STOP bullying,' and putting the hand up in this way signifies the stop."

Books like these enable young people to notice an escalation of hate when we treat behaviors on the lower levels of the Pyramid as "normal." Rather than accepting stereotypes or ignoring name-calling, students are motivated to ally behavior and to confronting oppression for a more just world. These attempts at deescalating hate are obvious in their insightful responses and in their understanding of a character's survival skills (textbox 6.1).

By the story's end, Lewis has learned lessons not only about identity and friendship but also about poverty as a relative term. Armed with experiential learning and embracing his Uncle Albert's words, "Can't let your fears get the best of you, isn't it? . . . Gotta live the best way you can" (p. 272), Lewis' desire for escape dissipates.

TEXTBOX 6.1: HOW TO BE LEWIS

Have a single mother who's struggling to make ends meet.
Belong to the Tuscarora Tribe and hold the key element for cultural preservation:
speaking your native language
but cut your braid because you desperately hope to fit in.
Exhibit eagerness to succeed in the "white man's" educational system and to explore unknown territory.
Share a deep intimacy for Paul McCartney's music and
build a friendship based upon a common love for that music.
Suffer from the torment of a bully's hands but
refuse to accept others' concepts on thinking.
Despite misconceptions, prove your worth by
braving the dangers of reality.
—College Freshman

As students engage dialogically to discuss this literature, teachers can encourage them to question an author's or speaker's assumptions and premises. They can assess the veracity of the claims and the soundness of the reasoning, using life experience and additional research to confirm or refute the text. By citing specific evidence and supporting their points in writing and speaking, students experience the rigor, critical thinking, and communication skills prized by the Common Core State Standards (CCSS). While the CCSS specifically state a mandate for exploring multiple viewpoints, there is reasonable concern that they also minimize the importance of YAL. However, these books meet the critical components required by the CCSS while also appealing to readers.

Discussions of CIL might take place in a literature circle format. Literature circles are temporary discussion groups whose members have chosen to read the same book or who have chosen to read different titles but on a similar topic, subject, or theme. The discussion engages every member of a small group as equal and active partners in sharing ideas and constructing interpretations in the reading process. The main focus in literature circles is group interaction: debate, challenge, and give-and-take to build on shared ideas and interpretations. Some of the following prompts may invite dialogic exchange during literature circles:

1. In what ways does this text incorporate or reflect aspects of your own life? To what aspects do you especially relate or connect?
2. To what extent does this text help build an understanding of culturally diverse people?
3. How might the text express ironies or contradictions of popular beliefs regarding the people of this culture?
4. How does the text connect in theme and content with other works of literature?
5. How might this text compare or conflict with the stories mainstream writers often tell?
6. Comment on how this text represents the cultural, historical, or social diversity of the people it attempts to depict. Where does or doesn't the author "get it right"?

With such prompts used in lively discussion, readers scrutinize the eleven identity elements and how they apply. While many educators prefer authentic discussion, where students lead with their own questions, concerns, and wonderings, a teacher might wish to explicitly employ the GREEN APPLE acronym to generate thought by predesigning questions as talking points. Those in textbox 6.2 provide a springboard for discussion.

Readers can also use the acronym as a scaffold to explore their reading, considering the role that gender, religion, economic class/socioeconomic status, ethnicity and race, name/family, age, perception of belonging, place, language, and exceptionality play in a text. The acronym encourages readers to focus on what otherwise might be invisible.

> **TEXTBOX 6.2: USING THE ACRONYM**
>
> G = How does gender identity contribute to the novel? What gender boundaries, if any, are placed on Lewis and on George? If gender is a social construct, what gender definitions exist in the novel?
>
> R = Consider the role music plays in the novel. In what ways, if any, is music tied to ritual and/or ceremony? How does music affect or influence Lewis' mind, body, and spirit? How might music foster cultural awareness or enhance one's heritage?
>
> E = What happens when Lewis tries to make friends at his new school with the teasing ways he used at his reservation school? Explain the conflict Lewis has about cutting his braid. How does George's German heritage play a role in the story? What motivates Lewis' desire for "skin bleach"? Why/How might skin color privilege or challenge a person? What social customs of the Tuscarora Indian does Lewis practice? In what German social practices and customs does the Haddonfield family engage?
>
> E = What conditions account for the class differences in the life lived by Lewis and that lived by George? How do their identities compare or contrast with your own socioeconomic status?
>
> N = What might the author be communicating about Lewis by withholding his name until page 59 of the novel?
>
> A = Mostly, this is a book about adolescents, but it also gives glimpses into the life lived by Uncle Albert and other adults. How does Lewis' age contribute to or account for some of his challenges in life? What role does Uncle Albert play in Lewis' life?
>
> P = Why might celebrating the U.S. Bicentennial not be a priority on the reservation? Based on the novel's portrayal, what does it mean to live on the Tuscarora Reservation? On an Air Force base? What role does place play in shaping these two young men? In contrast or comparison, how has place shaped your identity?

P = Why does Lewis resist being "that kid from the reservation"? Why does Lewis wish to be invisible when it suits him? What barriers does Lewis identify in his search for friendship?

L = How does Lewis' knowing his native language, Tuscarora, both complicate and enhance his life? Uncle Albert's speaking patterns capture some of the local flavor of language on the Tuscarora Reservation: "Can't let your fears get the best of you, isn't it?" (p. 272). What idioms are culturally relevant to you?

E = The book discusses issues of being enrolled in an advanced class, of Lewis' being a brainiac. How does this label both privilege and/or hinder his life? How do labels like this or other exceptionalities function in society?

The acronym works with any book because it encourages focus on key cultural identity markers and facilitates the construction of new knowledge as readers expand their schemata for a richer understanding of diversity.

In another title from the CIL list, *Up to This Pointe*, author Jennifer Longo (2016) develops a rich plot with interesting characters from whom readers can learn important life lessons while guided by GREEN APPLE questions (see resource 6.2 at the end of this chapter). She also invites readers to engage with her characters, to experience "a truth informed by facts, but not made up entirely of them" (Author's Note), and to explore the question: What would I do if this were happening to me?

Staying determined, disciplined, and driven, Harper Scott and her best friend, Kate Grey, have been working since before preschool on their goal: To dance with the San Francisco Ballet Company. Thinking that sacrifices, motivation, dedication, passion, and effort will ensure success, Harper doesn't believe in luck. Motivated by those thoughts, she is chasing fulfillment.

Because Harper is also a descendant of Robert Falcon Scott, the Englishman who is best known for his legendary and fatal attempt to be the first to reach the South Pole, she has adopted a motto: "Succeed, or die in the attempt" (p. 13). With Scott in her blood, Roald Amundsen in her will, and Ernest Shackleton contributing endurance vibes, Harper intends to plant her flag. Harper's brother, Luke—named for the Star Wars character—sees the hard work and the passion in his sister, and calls her his Yoda, his hero who emulates the motto: "Do or do not. There is no try" (p. 147).

Now, at seventeen and with auditions imminent, Harper and Kate are about to see their faithful efforts come to fruition—only they don't, and Harper is left to make sense of what she considers a ruined life.

Numb, disappointed, and disillusioned, Harper wishes to escape to Antarctica so that she can be alone and embrace the darkness that overwhelms her. After applying for a National Science Foundation grant for seniors looking to enrich their science education, Harper secures a position—with some string pulling and some stretching of the truth—as the research assistant of Charlotte, a biology student doing penguin research under Ellen Scott, a marine biology professor who is also Charlotte's thesis advisor and Harper's mother.

However, Harper doesn't belong to the discourse community of scientists. The language she knows especially well is that spoken by ballet dancers: pointe shoes, rond de jambe turns, grand jetés, battements, and pliés. But under Charlotte's tutelage, Harper falls in love with the Adélie penguins and learns to think in questions. Despite her attempts to turn what she thinks she knows over and over, to discover what's underneath, to let herself be surprised, and to see life from a new angle and in a new light, Harper remains lost, defining herself by what she lacks.

Depressed, grieving, and colder than she's ever been before, Harper begins to show signs of T3, a thyroid condition that affects cognitive sharpness and plunges a person into a fugue state as the brain reassigns chemicals to keep the body warm and alive. With a prescription to make frequent visits to the McMurdo Station greenhouse, Harper lies in a hammock where Shackleton, a principal figure in the Heroic Age of Antarctic Exploration, gets inside her head.

These hallucinations help Harper focus on changes in thinking and behavior. Shackleton's candor forces Harper to consider disappointment, entitlement, and her gifts from new angles. Letters from home in San Francisco—especially those from Owen and Willa—and insight from Vivian, Charlotte's other lab assistant, further assist Harper in cataloging what she considers the ruins of her life. Aiden Kelly also serves as an attentive suitor and distraction on Antarctica as Harper moves through the stages of grief. Gradually, she comes to understand Shackleton's wisdom: "You will the truth you need to survive; you make it so" (p. 212).

Like feet in satin pointe shoes, Harper is so swaddled in agony that it takes going to Antarctica for her to thaw, for her to learn the important distinction between *difficult* and *impossible*: "one requires a huge amount of effort.... And the other requires more" (p. 332). She also learns to forgive and to trust herself, to accept that no set of goals and objectives includes every situation, and to revise her life story for a better ending.

Often, students' first observation about Longo's protagonist is "What an obsessive-compulsive personality!" or "What a fanatic!" Their responses are ripe for investigation and invite critical thinking with potential to expand psychological schemata. Using the questions in textbox 6.3 after calling a CEO alert will enable learners not only to explore how a therapist diagnoses an obsessive-compulsive disorder but to think about labels and the names we assign to people, places, and things.

Unless we stop to think about these labels and their potentially insidious results, we may be oblivious to their effects. When we categorize people, for example, these labels put them into boxes, and no matter what they do or say, our psychological schemata won't let them out of that box. The label defines them. Instead of seeking to understand any differences, we might use the differences to put a wall around the person. We don't objectively look at their behavior or their value set and try to understand it; we just make our summary statement and place that person in their box.

Interrogation of our labels and our labeling practices, as well as exposure to increase awareness, might open our minds so that we can also open the boxes in which we've trapped ourselves or others. Through Harper Scott, Longo teaches readers how jumping out of our boxes and shredding our labels leads to discovery.

TEXTBOX 6.3: QUESTIONS TO EXPAND PSYCHOLOGICAL SCHEMATA

1. What does it mean to be ____ (insert whatever label learners are using)?
2. List as many synonyms as you can for the term ____. How is this word related to the term normal?
3. Evaluate the behavior of one of the novel's protagonists; what words would you use to describe that character's actions and motivations? Why did you choose these words? Do these terms fairly and accurately assess this person?
4. Through the lens of normal, evaluate Longo's protagonist's dedication to a Plan and her admonishment of luck as bullshit (25), her reaction to her setback, her choice to travel to Antarctica, and any other behaviors about which you are curious.

In the spirit of pairing a young adult novel with a classic text, teachers might consider T. S. Eliot's dramatic monologue "The Love Song of J. Alfred Prufrock," a poem in which the persona has been judged and fixed by "a formulated phrase." Eliot's poem serves as an appropriate companion text for interrogating not only how names can shape attitudes but how others are affected by our labels. With this poem, Eliot, who was twenty-two when he penned most of Prufrock, wrote a pointed attack on well-dressed, moneyed, and sophisticated citizens with a preference for material pleasures over genuine human interaction. These facts make the poem one that young adults will likely find relevant and relatable.

After all, we construct meanings that are influenced by who we are and what we are culturally, socially, historically, and psychologically. Our different backgrounds and orientations will produce different interpretations because these personal experiences provide the lenses that color our reading of a text—whether that be a billboard, a television episode or commercial, a film, a newspaper, a magazine, a poem, or a facial expression.

We can correct our vision and sharpen our sight by remembering that gender identity, religion, socioeconomic status/class, ethnicity and race, name/family, age, place/geography, perception of belonging, and exceptionality all shape our cultural identities. These factors not only influence and impose limitations on what we see because of our parochialism but can potentially enrich how we read the world, how we respond to others, and how we live our lives.

With all the curves life throws and the obstacles it presents, sometimes we can feel like all we're doing is dodge dancing. During such confusing, frustrating, and difficult times, we need a how-to manual. We can find this operational knowledge not only by reading the world around us with questions inspired by the GREEN APPLE acronym as a guide but also by reading about others who have lived challenging lives and found ways to survive. Reading through the GREEN APPLE lenses can unlock thoughts and open spaces in our minds where we can later return, to rummage and reflect on what we've learned.

All students will benefit if we take the time to learn about one another. Cultural Identity Literature and dialogic exchange guided by the GREEN APPLE acronym aren't panaceas, but as learning tools they do encourage cultural border crossing, seeing from multiple perspectives, challenging dominant modes of knowing, and producing knowledge from facts. With such bridge-building, hopefully we can mitigate human cruelty and the tendency to hate, reject, or ignore what one doesn't know or even try to understand.

Because some things are invisible until they happen to us, we may be blind to ignorance and hate as diseases until we are victims or until a story opens our eyes. About education, Robert Frost said: "Education is the ability to listen to almost anything without losing your temper or your self-confidence." As young people engage in open-minded discussion, the goal is to achieve this level of education, to understand that difference isn't a defect and that there are many ways of thinking, feeling, believing, and behaving.

With CIL, we begin to develop a culturally responsive mindset, a mindset that embraces alternate perspectives, is open to new ways of knowing, and recognizes the value of looking beyond the self. CRS honors, respects, and uses students' identities and backgrounds as meaningful sources for creating optimal learning environments.

Just as readers transform a text as they read, bringing diverse understandings of literary conventions to the reading, these conventions have potential to transform readers, informing them as they respond to textual encounters. Reading with a GREEN APPLE guide and being open to the inquiry process will not only build the bridges needed for cultural border crossing but will encourage readers to imagine another way to see.

The list of CIL titles shared in this book's appendix is not intended to be an exhaustive or a privileged list. It simply lists books that have been used with efficacy in secondary and post-secondary classrooms. Educators who agree with novelist Adichie (2009) about "the danger of the single story" with its ability to rob a people of its dignity will likely also agree that classrooms and bookshelves need to reflect a range of CIL. No single text can carry the burden of representing a diverse population, and no single text can provide the important triad of experiences outlined by children's literature specialist Rudine Sims Bishop (1990), offering windows, sliding glass doors, and mirrors.

Cultural Identity Literature titles enable readers to see other people's experiences, to walk into worlds they might not otherwise have imagined, and to see their own experiences reflected back at them. Reading, discussing, and writing about diverse literary narratives offers the opportunity to cultivate what Martha Nussbaum (1996) calls the narrative imagination.

When we become good readers of someone else's story, we not only begin to see our own lives and experiences as part of the larger human experience, but we come to empathize with those individuals, and empathy is one key to understanding. The act of reading many stories has the power to form and to transform readers. Once we begin to think differently, hopefully behavior will follow and we can find connection as humans.

Educators should not fixate about those students who appear staunch in their opinions. As this chapter suggests, the process of constructing new knowledge so as to enlarge and revise psychological schema and scripts may be long and difficult. Furthermore, there are some things from which some of us can never fully escape any more than we can escape ourselves.

However, any seeds we plant will not be futile work for the sower. These seeds may lie dormant for many years until they are watered by new experiences or until the learner reaches that point of readiness and begins to look beneath the surface of people, recognizing that substance needs to backup strong emotion.

RESOURCE 6.1: RATIONALE MODEL

Title: *And Tango Makes Three*
Author: Peter Parnell and Justin Richardson
Awards/Critical Acclaim:
National Book Awards

- American Library Association Notable Children's Book, 2006
- ASPCA's Henry Bergh Award, 2005
- Gustavus Myer Outstanding Book Award, 2006
- Nick Jr. Family Magazine Best Book of the Year, 2006
- Bank Street Best Book of the Year, 2006
- Cooperative Children's Book Council Choice, and CBC/NCSS Notable Social Studies Trade Book, 2006
- Lambda Literary Award finalist, 2006

Awards from Children's Groups

- Living the Dream Book Award, 2007, given by the fifth graders of Manhattan Country School, Children's Workshop School, and Central Park East II
- Sheffield Children's Book Award, shortlisted, 2008

Objectives (pedagogical and philosophical explanations/connections): Students will

- Receive exposure to the notion of same-sex parent families.
- Learn what it means to feel included and to matter.
- Develop an awareness about marginalization.
- Recognize that plants and animals go through predictable life cycles that include birth, growth, development, reproduction, and death.
- Understand that personal and family differences should be respected.
- Discuss different family structures, inclusive of families of diverse cultures and persuasions.

Plot Description: The book is based on the true story of Roy and Silo, two male Chinstrap Penguins in New York's Central Park Zoo who for six years formed a couple. The book follows part of this time in the penguins' lives. The pair are observed trying to hatch a rock that resembles an egg. When zookeepers realize that Roy and Silo are both male, it occurs to them to give them an egg to hatch. A second egg is obtained from a male-female penguin couple that had previously been unable to successfully hatch two eggs at once. As a family, Roy and Silo hatch and raise the healthy young chick, a female named "Tango" by keepers.

Strategies for Addressing Sensitive Issues: Due to the penguin parents being of the same sex, some people object to children reading/hearing the book. The natural existence of homosexuality in animals is considered controversial by conservative religious groups who oppose LGBTQ social movements because these findings seem to point to the natural occurrence of homosexuality in humans. Whether this has logical or ethical implications is also a source of debate, with some arguing that it is illogical to use animal behavior to justify what is or is not moral for humans.

The authors are not arguing in favor of human gay relationships; they simply wish to help parents teach about same-sex parent families. Senior penguin keeper Mr. Gramzay said that he never saw the pair complete a sex act, but the two did engage in mating rituals like entwining their necks and vocalizing to one another.

Alternate Selections

Skin Again by bell hooks
This book celebrates all that makes us unique and different. It offers new ways to talk about race and identity. Race matters, but only so much—what's most important is who we are on the inside. Looking beyond skin, going straight to the heart, we find in each other the treasures stored down deep. Learning to cherish those treasures, to be all we imagine ourselves to be, makes us free. *Skin Again* celebrates this freedom and supports us on our journey for acceptance.

Sometimes My Mommy Gets Angry by Bebe Moore Campbell
This book is an excellent means to introduce the concept of mental illness to children, particularly bipolar disorder. Narrated from a child's perspective, it presents symptoms and coping strategies in simple, everyday terms, and gently opens a door for serious discussion. From this book, we learn how love can prevail despite mental illness. When we explore untouchable and unspoken territory, we find spaces for acceptance and learn to redefine normalcy.

RESOURCE 6.2

Using the GREEN APPLE Acronym with *Up to This Pointe*

Gender: What is your reaction to Ben's behavior? Why does Harper call Ben *the Beard*? What do you make of Char-

Chapter Six

lotte's categorization of people on Antarctica on page 40 and of Aiden's commentary about "lady books" on page 117? If gender is a social construct, what other gender definitions exist in the novel?

Religion: Reflect on what you know or have heard about church and religion. Explain how your experiences and understandings might compare or align more with Harper's reaction to Scott's Hut on page 42 or to Aiden's term Cafeteria Catholic on page 204 or to the Chapel of the Snows on page 333? What might worshipping at The Altar of Keeping Warm mean? How might ballet be like a religion? Consider the description Harper shares on page 25 as a starting point.

Economic Class: What details give clues about the socioeconomic class to which Owen, Kate, and Harper each belong? How do these identities compare or contrast with your own socioeconomic status?

Ethnicity/Race: How does the description of the Chinese New Year celebration on pages 270–79 align with or differ from your understanding and experiences? Consider how ethnicity shapes one's worldview. For a starting point, reread Owen's description on pages 309–11 about attending Chinese school where the values learned differed from those practiced at home. How is Harper's cutting her hair both similar to and different from the practice of some Indian tribes (p. 332)? For what purpose might Aiden be using the clichéd Irish jokes on his radio show? See pages 91 or 244 as examples. What descriptive details does the author use to indicate the racial identities of Charlotte, Owen, and Kate? Discuss the affirmative action comment on page 41 and consider other ways that skin color privileges or challenges a person. Why might Owen's mom object to a white girlfriend but "be in love with [Harper]" (p. 276)?

Name/Family: How do Harper's ancestors influence her behavior and shape who she is becoming? What expectations, reputation, unearned privileges, or limitations, if any, does Harper experience because of her family's name?

Age: How does age help to define behavior? Besides their age, what do Aiden, Owen, Luke, Charlotte, Kate, Vivian, and Harper all have in common? How does

	their adolescence contribute to or account for some of their challenges in life? Why might their career choices conflict with their parents' ideas? Consider Owen's parents' desire that he become a doctor and his own realization that he "also really [loves] sitting around in [his] boxer shorts playing *Halo*" (p. 276).
Place/Geography:	How do place and location contribute to and shape behavior? Consider Harper from San Francisco, Vivian from Minnesota, and Aiden from Ireland as transplants at McMurdo Station. How has place shaped your identity?
Perception of Belonging:	What happens when Harper hitches her identity and self-perception to being a dancer with the San Francisco Ballet Company? What are the consequences of looking for self-esteem and self-worth beyond the self?
Language:	Because each belongs to a unique discourse community with its own vernacular, what differences do you notice in the languages that are spoken by Harper, Charlotte, or Harper's dad? Consider the discourse community to which you belong; what vernacular/language is common to you?
Exceptionality:	Who is Benjamin Button, and why does Mr. Scott call his daughter Harper that on page 19? How does Kate embody giftedness? In your answer, consider Kate's "endless extension, every turn precise, perfectly executed. Her pointe shoes make no sound, even landing jetés [p. 10]. . . . Kate is what we aspire to. She is perfection" (p. 102). How do labels like *perfect, normal,* and *weird* function in society?

Chapter Seven

Pause and Ponder Moments

The art of using books to aid people in solving the issues they are facing is called bibliotherapy. First used in the United States in 1916 by Samuel Crothers, bibliotherapy has been the subject of considerable research since that time. Multiple researchers (Rasinki & Padak, 1990; Becker, Pehrsson, & McMillen, 2008; Shechtman, 2009) have shown that literary fiction enhances our ability to empathize with others, to put ourselves into another's shoes, to become more intuitive about other people's feelings (as well as our own), and to self-reflect on our problems as we read about and commiserate with fictional characters who are facing similar problems.

According to Bucher and Hinton (2013), our minds and our imaginations are more engaged when reading than when watching films because we need to fill in so much that is not specifically put into words, in other words, to make inferences.

Making inferences is a key ability that students must employ to read, write, speak, listen, and use language effectively in a variety of content areas, as well as for college, career, and community readiness. In an effort to promote the literacy skills and concepts required for this readiness in multiple disciplines, the Common Core State Standards (2018) speak frequently to what Marzano (2010) calls a "foundational skill," one that is a prerequisite not only for reading comprehension but for higher-order thinking.

Reasoned comprehension cannot happen without inferencing, a fact that likely explains why the first anchor standard for reading states that students should be able to "Read closely to determine what the text says explicitly and to make logical inferences from it; cite specific textual evidence when writing or speaking to support conclusions drawn from the text" (n.p.). For first graders through seniors in high school, the reading standards focus on students' ability to read carefully and grasp information, arguments, ideas, and details based on evidence in a text.

Author, librarian, and educator Judith Halsted (1994) recommends that leaders accompany readers on their inference-making journeys. She describes bibliotherapy as progressing through three phases: identification, catharsis, and insight. Teachers, school counselors, and librarians are positioned to serve as these leaders, not only to make a book recommendation that might dispense healing but to ask questions that encourage adolescents to investigate, clarify, and validate their feelings.

Furthermore, sociocultural theory suggests that youth naturally—and often effortlessly—develop competence by engaging in dialogue and shared activity with more experienced members (Vygotsky, 1978).

A simple yet effective strategy for encouraging this investigation, clarification, and validation is a learning tool called the Pause and Ponder Moment. The Pause and Ponder Moment is a strategy for reading all texts, not just those that might perform as bibliotherapy. Pause and Ponder Moments invite readers to stop, question, and reflect. What does the text say, what does it mean, and why does that/doesn't that matter are the core questions in Pause and Ponder Moments, although the questions can change as they are tailored to match each literary encounter.

These moments also carry promise for enriching how we read the world, how we respond to others, and how we live our lives. Because they impose reflection time, Pause and Ponder Moments reinforce reading as a deliberate and patient process. Imposing time to pause and think through points and concepts enables readers to truly grapple with content in meaningful ways. Pause and Ponder Moments further inspire attributional retraining and option awareness, alternatives to simply accepting the status quo.

Educators should likewise be aware that although literature has powers to heal, it also has limitations. For example, it cannot cure someone's emotional illness, it cannot guarantee that readers will behave in socially appropriate ways, and it cannot directly solve problems. Situations like these require intervention, sometimes by skilled therapists.

PAUSE AND PONDER MOMENTS

Any occasion in a text that invites interrogation makes a good Pause and Ponder Moment. Readers might ask questions about the caustic effects of shame, for example, and how shame and guilt can erode one's self-esteem and produce devastating results. When shame results in self-attack or self-harm, it negatively colors how we view ourselves and how we assess the prospect of recovering our self-esteem. Talking about shame, its triggers and its effects, not only sheds light on this often taboo topic but potentially lessens the power it has over our lives.

Another strategy for esteem building is to separate what we do from our sense of self-worth. Psychologist Gershen Kaufman (1996) writes about re-growing one's identity with self-affirmation and through active imagery, which involves "the process of reowning and reparenting a part of yourself previously shamed and disowned" (p. 216). Because our insecurities frequently give rise to shame, an exercise to assist in the re-owning and re-parenting process invites students to name something about themselves that they would change if they could. Following that naming, the activity invites the writing of statements of homage, praising and celebrating that previously criticized or despised trait or condition.

As a model, a teacher might read Lucille Clifton's poem "homage to my hips" (1987), which defies the popular European conception that big-hipped women are less appealing than those who are slender hipped. This poem often gives rise to a conversation about how opinion gets recycled and restated until it is popularized, so teachers may wish to lead a discussion about how human beings construct meanings that are influenced by who we are and what we are culturally, socially, historically, and psychologically.

Our different backgrounds and orientations will produce different interpretations of life encounters because these personal experiences provide the lenses that color our reading of a text—whether that be a billboard, a television episode or commercial, a film, a newspaper, a magazine, a novel, a facial expression, or one's body image.

We can adjust our vision and sharpen our sight by remembering that gender identity, religion, ethnicity and race, economic class/socioeconomic status, name/family, age, place (national territory/geography), perception of belonging, and exceptionality—whether gifted or challenged—(GREEN APPLE) all shape our cultural identities and can potentially enrich how we read the world, how we respond to others, and how we live our lives.

Deconstruction, what educational researcher Deborah Appleman (2009) calls "a particular kind of unbuilding" (p. 99), inspires scrutiny and questions; it helps adolescents see the limits of binary thinking, like fat—thin. Taking into account all the elements that compose a constructed message requires the rigor of close reading. Another benefit of this multiple-perspective approach is that such viewing enables students to exercise mental flexibility; it informs reading by giving a sociocultural context.

According to Moroccan activist Fatema Mernissi, in Morocco, a woman with wide hips and a few extra pounds has always been the essence of beauty. Performing such research and analysis not only boosts knowledge construction and illustrates the power of multiple perspectives; it supplies a framework to critique and resist prevailing ideologies and to find more agreeable definitions and understandings.

Because body image is often rooted in one's desire to be attractive, a Pause and Ponder Moment on this topic might invite questions like: What does attractive mean? How did that definition come to be popular/prevalent? Who does that definition include and who does it leave out? The idea is to see exceptions to behavioral rules or social norms and to recognize other ways of knowing, even if this new thinking defies "popular opinion."

Rather than fixating on butts, boobs, or being fat, a fixation which actually objectifies and dehumanizes us, we can encourage young people to be the best versions of themselves by re-owning their identities with self-affirmation. Although staying silent may seem like the politically correct choice—minding your own business—putting your own need to be comfortable above the needs of someone in crisis may be a dangerous and irresponsible choice. Before a crisis occurs, we may need to share the reminder that suicide is a permanent solution to a temporary problem or to ask the question, "What are you doing with your hate?"

While the basic intention of political correctness encourages tact, respect for diversity, and sensitivity to others' feelings around issues such as gender identity, religion, ethnicity and race, economic class/socioeconomic status, name/family, age, place (national territory or geography), perception of belonging, and exceptionality—whether gifted or challenged—the effect of political correctness has virtually made these topics taboo.

Rather than constraining any meaningful discussion on diversity issues, we need to open the dialogue, not only to enlighten and to build knowledge but to interrupt the hate that results in oppression, racism, and other discriminatory attitudes and actions. Silence is not an effective strategy; it is actually hindering our ability to develop comfort in living and working with those who are different from us—we need to talk about diversity issues so that we can cross lines of difference.

Unfortunately, tolerance and political correctness have become problematic when they were initially intended to address social injustice. Because nothing can be changed unless it is first acknowledged, teachers can lead the charge by inviting conversation about tough topics into the classroom. When they do, they explore the effects of binary thinking, perform myth-busting, and promote social justice. In this way, books can perform bibliotherapy, with the therapeutic effects being attitude adjustment, perspective taking, and perspective making.

When nascent readers read, they often jump to conclusions about characters, events, or places. So, before reading a passage or a text in which this conclusion jumping may occur, teachers should remind readers to develop an attitude like that described by John Dewey (1910), one of "suspended conclusion." This willingness to be uncertain for a while as they navigate unfamiliar territory guards them against inaccurate evaluation. In making an inference or forming a judgment—especially a first impression—we typically rely on past experiences or encounters to help us name behavior: right—wrong, good—bad, normal—abnormal, proper—improper.

Many of these snap judgments carry a moral or psychological shortcut that is laden with cognitive bias. With these mental shortcuts, we have to be cautious and remember the exceptions. Just as with medicine, not all bodies respond to the same treatment; what is sometimes true isn't always true. In fact, we should spend a lifetime refining broad categories like these because such binaries virtually limit thinking. After all, first impressions can change and exceptions to parochial thinking do exist.

Teachers can open such textual moments with a simple Pause and Ponder exercise by asking students: What term would you use to describe this character or this individual? And what causes you to choose that term? With that data collected, learners hold a discussion, challenging one another to explain as clearly as they can why characters or some individuals behave as they do and whether any conventions, cultural codes, or personal behavior patterns are guiding their behavior. This exercise enables readers to determine whether they have fairly and accurately assessed an individual.

Learners might also think critically about labels, like girl or boy, and the other names we assign to people, places, and things. In a Pause and Ponder Moment, we can stop to think about these labels. As discussed in chapter 6, labels can be both inaccurate and even insidious.

When students respond to a text or to one another with ethnocentric, sexist, racist, or some other box-like response, teachers might invite them to think of the experience from the perspective of a traveler visiting another country. As they journey into the novelist's or another's world and take a look around, they might encounter a place where people's attitudes, opinions, and beliefs are very different from their own. Encouraging them to withhold judgment and to be curious about unfamiliarity and difference might give them the eyes of an explorer.

Unless we adopt such curiosity when we perform cultural border crossings or historical border crossings or any other crossings, we are setting ourselves up for disappointment or disillusionment. That willingness to be disturbed needs to accompany all learning.

As a Pause and Ponder exercise to assist students in appreciating the limitations of sight, teachers might invite them to engage in a viewing activity with a paper cup. Using a sharp object to make a hole no bigger than a dime in the bottom of a paper cup and then positioning the drinking end over one's eye will limit what the viewer can see. Invite participants to take a couple of "snapshots" and to describe in detail what is within their view, realizing how such limitations enable them to sharpen their focus, to really see something when the distractions are removed. Then, we talk about what is just out of our vision and what we don't see when we hone in on something or when we "see what we want to see."

Chapters 1 and 2 proposed that classroom teachers lead the way in correcting any vision impairments by offering diverse groups the opportunity to learn about each other. Such learning will involve confronting issues of power and privilege that dominate current social practices, asking questions about our world, seeing beyond stereotypes, and welcoming alternate ways of knowing and being. Preconceived notions about such subjects as gender, ability, and beauty affect not only how we react to others but also how we see them.

Difference is often a characteristic targeted by bullies. Readers can use the Pause and Ponder Moment strategy to discuss bullying or any other negative behavior and the actions a bystander might take in such a situation. Discussed in chapter 5, the Action Continuum with its eight stages of response from Actively Participating to Initiating Change and Advocating Prevention builds awareness about actions for inclusion and social justice and applies as a tool for such reflection.

From these metacognitive moments, readers gain knowledge. Because tough topic questions are mildly threatening and simultaneously harmless, they work to nudge learning into what developmental psychologist Lev Vygotsky (1978) termed the "Zone of Proximal Development" (ZPD). Vygotsky called the difference between what a child can do with help and what he or she can do without guidance the ZPD. Targeting the ZPD maximizes the odds that students will stay interested and alert because such moments create disequilibrium.

Vygotsky and other psychologists have shown that cognitive disequilibrium stimulates inquiry, curiosity, thinking, and deep questioning—actions that, in turn, lead to deeper learning. The wobble occurs when there are contradictions, conflicts, anomalous events, breakdown scenarios, obstacles to goals, salient gaps in knowledge, uncertainty, equally attractive alternatives, and other types of impasses. When these impasses occur, the learner needs to engage in reasoning, deeper thinking, problem solving, and planning in route to restoring cognitive equilibrium.

As students engage in dialogue and co-produce meaning, they learn that critical thinking comes only after they move beyond the tenacity of individual will, beyond influences from family, church, peer group, social convention, or law, and beyond justification toward a pre-determined outcome. Not rooted in mere feeling or long-held opinion, critical thinking requires actually having evidence to substantiate belief. Learning to think critically requires considerable teacher facilitation because students will resist the discomfort of uncertainty. A feeling of being lost or confused accompanies this productive learning, and learners who are disinclined to endure disorientation will require help to manage the learning wobble and to reach a level of more scientific reasoning.

Because we don't welcome the feeling of inadequacy that doubt brings, we may grab onto the first viable explanation or solution to stop the discomfort engendered by doubt. Even though doubt triggers the desire to discover, it can also cause a premature shutdown of the inquiry process.

Until students learn to welcome confusion as part of the learning process and until they grow confident in the stages of critical thinking, they will require nurturing and frequent nudging to challenge miscues, stereotypes, or off-track thinking: "How do you know? What evidence can you offer? Why do you think that? What might be another way to think?" This way the teacher can manage the conversation and invite students to imagine another way to see. It is for these reasons that Vygotsky likely included the caveat that such conversations are most effective when youth engage with more experienced members to develop competence. Without these experienced guides, nascent learners might not persist through the wobble.

In developing this competence, students might read texts from this book's appendix list of Cultural Identity Literature (CIL), any of the titles listed in resource 2.6, or those in chapter 4 to investigate contemporary social conditions and to critically examine the culture that created those conditions. Questions like those in textbox 7.1—questions that were developed primarily for social protest literature—provide a place to start as students explore what sociologist Helen Fein (1979) calls one's *universe of obligation*. These questions can easily be modified to align with the literature being read.

According to Fein, how the members of a group, a nation, or a community define who belongs and who does not has a lot to do with how they define their *universe of obligation*. Although Fein uses the phrase to describe the group of individuals within a society "toward whom obligations are owed, to whom rules apply, and whose injuries call for amends" (p. 4), we might also refer to an *individual's* universe of obligation.

This connection is enhanced by applying Urie Bronfenbrenner's (1979) Ecological Systems Theory, images of which are readily available online. Influenced by fellow developmental psychologist Lev Vygotsky, Bronfenbrenner theorized that numerous institutions and settings—including social, political, and economic conditions—interact and affect the developing

> **TEXTBOX 7.1: UNIVERSE OF OBLIGATION QUESTIONS**
>
> 1. Who are the individuals and groups that you feel you owe an obligation?
> 2. What factors influence how you define your universe of obligation?
> 3. In what ways might an individual communicate who is part of his/her universe of obligation and who is not?
> 4. What are the consequences when a breakdown in the universe of obligation occurs?
> 5. How might this breakdown contribute to prejudiced attitudes and to an escalation of hate if left unchecked?
> 6. When read through the lens of social protest literature, what social concern(s) does this text bring to light?
> 7. What contemporary evidence can you offer to support the author's/text's position?
> 8. What social conditions contribute to this issue of concern?
> 9. What strategies does the author employ for eliciting emotional and moral engagement by readers with characters in the novel?
> 10. What, if anything, can you do to improve the lives of marginalized individuals in your community?
> 11. What, if anything, can you do combat systemic racism?
> 12. What, if anything, might you need to unlearn in order to make room for new learning?
> 13. Although labels make the world smaller and more manageable, they also lead to preconceived notions. What assumptions might you need to struggle against?
> 14. What steps will you take in these growth processes?

human. Bronfenbrenner depicted these settings with interconnecting layers, from the most immediate environment—called the microsystem—to the connections that extend beyond family, peers, school, and community.

As we venture beyond these immediate environments, we encounter influences by local politics, industry, mass media, and various social services. Ultimately, we experience the influence of the most expansive system—the macrosystem—which is composed of dominant beliefs and practices derived from cultural values and ideologies as well as influences from broader political, social, and economic systems. Each of these ecological systems inevitably interact with and influence one another in all aspects of our lives.

Like ripples in a pond, Bronfenbrenner's model suggests that interactions between individuals and their environments shape personal development over time—the chronosystem.

To open a conversation about obligation, a teacher might invite students to sketch and label these universes. Once they have considered to whom they owe responsibility in their immediate environments, the teacher can suggest that students move beyond the family and friends circle to consider neighborhoods, communities, institutions, and other social systems to which they may feel an obligation. As students sketch and label these universes, the teacher might lead a discussion about factors that shape how we define our universe of obligation and the roles that cultural values and altruism play in restricting or enlarging this universe.

From this exercise, students often take away a key fact: Everything we do and think affects the people in our lives, and their reactions in turn affect others. Therefore, the choices we make have far-reaching consequences.

When we begin to see the world through these new eyes and to understand that each of us carries within us the capacity to change the world in small ways for better or for worse, we might also begin to view our obligations differently. Perhaps when we encounter prejudice, we might intervene and interrupt hurt, we might create conditions that reduce instances of injustice, or we might refuse to remain silent. Students who undergo such training will not only examine the borders suggested by Roiphe in chapter 6 but perhaps adopt Anna Sewell's stance in *Black Beauty*, that when we see cruelty and oppression, we need to intervene.

Another tool mentioned in chapter 6, using the Anti-Defamation League's Pyramid of Hate (2005) and applying the graphic to a novel or human social interaction enables learners to consider choices made by people in the past and to apply these strategies to guide their own words and actions for the future. In their daily interactions, individuals choose for themselves whether to act as a perpetrator, an ally, or a bystander when they encounter the bullying, microaggressions, and prejudices that continue to affect schools and communities today. Experiences in using the Pyramid enable young people to notice the effects of not speaking and to connect those outcomes to their silence.

The fight for justice and systemic change requires a powerful voice. We can't be silent, and we have to speak truth. We can all probably recall times when we laughed uncomfortably at someone's racist or homophobic comment. If we allow those moments to slide, such commentary becomes okay to the speaker and "normal" to those unjustly targeted. Every time we speak out against systemic racism or another social injustice and follow those words with actions, we are making strides toward greater altruism.

Sometimes, we need to help someone start a rough conversation, even if that person is an adult or our own parents. Racism is still around today—it's in the police force and in our families—so it is up to each one of us to tackle the tough topics posed by contemporary issues—issues like privilege, power, police violence, and prejudice.

If we don't talk about difficult issues like racism, nothing will change. If we make racist comments, like expecting a black person to know how to play basketball or to bake a sweet potato pie, and we don't recognize how such microaggressions accumulate and create deep wounds, then we're not embracing social justice. While the intention may not be to be racist or to hurt someone, saying the wrong thing is like the difference between bumping roughly into someone by mistake and intentionally ramming them. Only one is mean, but they both may hurt.

By talking about these differences and recognizing the hurt they cause, we can make progress. But not doing anything is a problem that won't get better because nothing changes. Although progress may bring some dark times, weathering those storms is better than not growing at all.

When we discover that what we say matters and that we can hurt people even when we don't mean to, we need to accept responsibility for overstepping our bounds and to figure out how to do better next time. We can't expect the offended person to make circumstances better for us.

We all benefit by growing wiser when we take the time to learn about one another. While using CIL as a catalyst for conversation isn't a panacea, it does serve as a learning tool that encourages seeing from multiple perspectives and challenging dominant modes of knowing. With such conversations, hopefully we can mitigate human cruelty and the tendency to hate, reject, or ignore what one doesn't know or even try to understand. Because some things are invisible until they happen to us, we may be blind to ignorance and hate as diseases until we are victims or until a story opens our eyes. Once our eyes are open, it is difficult to close them again.

Discussions stimulated by influential texts like those on the CIL list have the power to shift perspectives and to inspire lasting change. Learning about others has potential to make our eyes different; we begin to look beyond the self and one way of knowing and believing, to accept alternatives. These eye-opening stories give us the courage to speak out about people and issues that matter. They might also enable us to realize that equality and equity are two different concepts. While equality is treating everyone the same—as in equal pay for equal work—equity is taking difference into account so that everyone has a chance to succeed. The first one sounds fair but only the second one is.

To illustrate, consider how it is equal to assign the completion of ten math problems or the reading of twenty-five novel pages to all students, but if one of those students has an individualized education plan (IEP), the teacher may reduce the assignment as a modification or make an accommodation by giving the second student with an IEP access to an audio version of the novel.

ATTRIBUTIONAL RETRAINING

One college professor told the story about a time she directed a teacher training program, mentoring a cohort of preservice teachers. Occasionally one of them would come to her, exasperated about another professor's "demanding expectations" or a course's "unreasonable requirements." After listening to the student vent and offering commiseration, the professor would then say, "Now that you are aware of all of these demands, expectations, and requirements, how will you find a way to be successful?"

In this Pause and Ponder Moment, the student would engage in problem solving rather than in blaming. Such metacognition diverts energy into coping with life's difficult circumstances and putting the power back into personal hands. Students need multiple reminders that they are the authors of their own life stories and that the power to revise is also often in their hands.

When bad things happen—as they always will—we need to remember that it doesn't help to rage, to place blame, or simply to wish for alternate outcomes. Although we cannot bend the fabric of space and time and reality to get what we want, we can choose whether to allow the negativity to cause hurt or we can choose to take control.

When we dissect frustration or anger, we often find fear. An exercise that can help students to combat that fear—that insecurity that they might not be good enough—teachers might invite students to complete this sentence: I feel most powerful when ___. Next, students should compose a list of personal assets, titling the list *My Assets* so that the next time they feel disempowered, they can read the list as a form of what psychologists call "attributional retraining." In the classroom, we might close that listing exercise with a session of the Gratitude Game. As we go around the room and through the alphabet, each student in turn names something for which he/she is grateful, with each letter in the alphabet providing the prompt.

During times of confusion, frustration, and difficulty, we need a how-to manual. We can find this operational knowledge by seeking out or reading about others who have lived challenging lives and found ways to survive.

Young adult books and CIL hold potential to perform this attributional retraining, a process by which a person is led to reflect on his/her own attributions for a situation and to consider alternative explanations. For example, instead of thinking, "I'm not good enough" or "I'm the only one who's struggling," attributional retraining replaces unhelpful explanations about self-worth with explanations that will sustain self-esteem.

Reading about and discussing crisis situations helps people shift blame for negative events from "It's just me" to "I'm not alone; others share my struggles and find a way to survive." Such attributional retraining performs as acceptance intervention, which has the potential to downgrade uncontrollable stress by allowing people to put a narrative around their traumatic experiences. After reading and discussion, teachers might invite students to reflect upon their own crises and then to write about those experiences with a beginning, a middle, and a hopeful end. This nonthreatening framework provides a template for interpreting daily challenges—they can be boxed, scrutinized, and managed. This process can facilitate healing of the mind, body, and spirit.

Despite occasional heart-rending moments that plunge a reader to the depths of despair, reading invites us to ask important psychological questions, such as How do you fill your hole? We all occasionally experience feelings of emptiness, and how we choose to fill that hole and where we look to find fulfillment has immense importance for emotional, physical, and mental health. We can't look outside ourselves to find approval. With attributional retraining, we might see the value in channeling addictive or obsessive traits into creating, rather than in destroying.

Under the influence of such dialogue pedagogy, students banter, negotiate, weigh, and consider ideas proposed by contentious topics. In the process, they develop an enriched, multifaceted understanding of the concept discussed. A text's potential expands through their critical interpretation, under the scrutiny of shared insight and connections.

The teacher can also remind learners that the point of a discussion is for us to develop and grow as people. When our views are questioned, we can look at the situation as an opportunity to learn something new, as opposed to feeling defensive or combative.

With this learning model, students learn to listen through dialogue and to warrant their assertions. They come to realize that their arguments won't stand on emotion alone; they must be supported by facts. In the process, they grow wiser since wisdom depends on the examination of multiple perspectives, on researching different ways of knowing, and on accepting that personal understanding and experiences provide only one, limited viewpoint.

While some of these ideas might sound idealistic, teachers will often attempt to create conditions in their classrooms that might reflect the world in which they would like to live. With the help of this book, perhaps other classroom teachers will develop their own strategies for nurturing critical, creative, and curious thinkers who recognize that we're all programmed by our experiences and our pasts but that with free will we also have the ability to reprogram if we choose.

Although a legacy and memories of the past can serve us well, allowing them to define us or to limit our thinking without our consent can have dire consequences. Heritage is meant to provide inspiration, not become a box. When teachers initiate discussions that may disrupt readers' sense of comfort and when we challenge the status quo, we potentially make room for new learning.

The words of James Baldwin (2010) might provide inspiration as teachers take their students on their learning journeys: "Not everything that is faced can be changed. But nothing can be changed until it is faced" (p. 42).

PATIENCE IN THE REPROGRAMMING PROCESS

On this learning journey, when confronted with a revelation of new information, individuals will typically respond in one of two ways: either with discovery, awareness, and openness; or with fear, defensiveness, and anger. In the first mode, we are often curious, our minds open to knowledge and our hearts open to compassion. We may wonder, measuring this new idea against our paradigm of previous understanding. In this mode, we are able to withhold judgment as we struggle through the adventure of acceptance.

In the second, this new information threatens our long-held beliefs, giving us the sensation that we are no longer safe. We may respond to this discomfort with resistance, rejection, or even violence.

These two modes are common in the classroom where we often invite students to take risks. As new ideas bump up against established learning, similar to playing pinball, we knock away the ball. Intrigued, we can keep the ball in play, or we can walk away from the game.

According to the conventional wisdom in innovative fields, without the willingness to take risks—including the risk of failing—nothing of significance would ever be discovered (Miller, 2013). If achievement is about failure, then why in education is the possibility of an F worse than Hester's scarlet letter A? We are about as afraid of confusion as we are afraid of failure. These affective states are connected to our self-esteem and to our needs for mastery. We are taught to avoid these feelings, socialized into thinking they are taboo. Fear of failure often censors a person, who will do what's safe. Because we don't take risks or ask questions, we learn less.

Perhaps because of an educator's desire to recast failure as a learning tool, research like Thomas Newkirk's (2012) is intriguing. In a felicitous paradox, Newkirk explores the pleasures of difficulty and quotes Mike Rose: "Error marks the place where education begins" (p. 118). Achievement levels would rise if more students and teachers believed in the value of error.

Students often forget that learning is a gradual process requiring time and effort; for them understanding doesn't happen fast enough. They are surprised at their unknowing: "I don't understand," they will remark upon their initial encounter with Jonathan Swift's "A Modest Proposal" or their first attempt at doing a geometric proof. As novices, they don't yet know that the path to understanding is cluttered, digressive, and protracted; that understanding requires experience, dialectical practice, and intellectual habituation. An appropriate response to such impatience is, "You're not supposed to understand. Not yet."

Those two words suggest promise and potential. *Potential,* with its root word *potent,* means that there is energy or force for growth and development. Imagine the transformation that would occur if educators were to abolish the grades of D and F and replace them with NY—Not Yet. Instead of sending the demoralizing message of reprimand and failure, the NY suggests possibility—that given time, patient practice, and application, achievement will come. When a student says, "I don't get it," the nurturing "not yet" supports the notion of eventual competence.

Although the human mind resists confusion, from this feeling of disequilibrium, learning grows. Newkirk (2012) agrees, saying that intelligence measures derive from one's ability to work through the initial discomfort of situations that don't make sense: "Intelligence is not a matter of being smart—it is the capacity to view difficulty as an opportunity to stop, reassess, and employ strategies for making sense of problems" (p. 122).

These same habits of mind define reflection, a critical component in learning. A reflective learner is attentive and receptive while skeptical and focusing on meaning making. Dewey (1910) valued this skepticism and considered doubt essential to the thinking process, defining "the attitude of suspended conclusion" as "the most important factor in the training of good mental habits" (p. 13).

In his later scholarship, Dewey (1938) described reflection as the process of "[looking] back over what has been done so as to extract the net meanings which are the capital stock for intelligent dealing with further experiences" (p. 87). Although such reflection fosters critical thinking, getting learners to this point will require patient nurturing. The process will take time and repeated practice, and it will depend on the learner's readiness.

NORMALIZING CONFUSION

Teachers can begin this nurturing process by normalizing confusion. While fostering confusion seems to run contrary to education, learning actually begins in moments of disequilibrium. According to Wells (2009), "the key to teaching critical thinking effectively is to address doubt management" (p. 218). She describes how doubt, an irritating and uncomfortable state, provokes inquiry or investigation. Because we are motivated to return to belief—to a state of comfort—we might seek any answer, no matter how suspect, just to end the irritation of doubt.

Thinking is suspect unless we move beyond the tenacity (individual will), authority (influence from family, church, peer group, or law), and priority (decision in search of justification or directed toward a pre-determined outcome) levels in the thought process—eventually reaching the scientific level where we actually have evidence to substantiate belief. While doubt starts the process of investigation, it can also prematurely shut down inquiry. Therefore, true learning depends on our tolerance threshold, upon how long we can wrestle with doubt.

Blau (2003) refers to that same threshold as a "*willingness to suspend closure*—to entertain problems rather than avoid them" (p. 211). He claims that the major difference between less skilled and more productive learners is not about wit but about one's willingness to endure disorientation, that feeling of being lost or confused. Because Blau recognizes the role of confusion in developing critical thinking, he proposes the following principle: "Confusion often represents an advanced state of understanding [because] the student who is confused is frequently the one who understands enough to see a problem" (p. 21).

Based on this proposition, Blau advocates for curriculum designs that foster confusion: "In a classroom where intellectual problems and confusion are honored as rich occasions for learning, students and teachers will be more inclined to confront and even seek rather than avoid the textual and conceptual problems that offer the richest opportunities for learning" (p. 56).

So what impedes one's ability to manage doubt or to welcome confusion? Newkirk says it's the fear of embarrassment, that doing badly is less risky than admitting inadequacy by asking for help. Regardless of how thoroughly teachers present a lesson, they cannot anticipate and remove every confusion students may experience. Teachers depend on student questions as cues for additional scaffolding, but these questions often don't come. With their expertise, their polished products of research and training, teachers render confusion implausible.

Newkirk claims this "preparation may be a mask hiding the very process we want students to master" (p. 135); a failure to demonstrate uncertainty and confusion misrepresents learning. As an antidote, educators might consider modeling the initial false starts that come with learning. We can further normalize difficulty by asking questions like, where did you struggle and how are you working to solve those problems? While these questions may not make uncertainty enjoyable, at least we welcome the wobble as a typical guest in the learning process.

As another obstacle to critical thinking, Dweck (2010) names a fixed mindset. Students with a fixed mindset see ability as something inherent that needs to be demonstrated. They believe that intelligence is static—they only have a certain amount. Their desire to look smart leads to a tendency to avoid challenges, to give up easily, to see efforts as futile, to ignore useful feedback, and to feel threatened by the success of others. According to Dweck's earlier research (2008), those with a fixed mindset perceive "challenges, mistakes, and even the need to exert effort as threats to their ego rather than as opportunities to improve" (p. 36).

When students instead have a growth mindset, they understand that intelligence can be developed and doesn't depend on luck or genetics; rather, like a muscle, intelligence grows stronger through exercise. Instead of worrying about how smart they currently are, they work to improve by embracing challenges, persisting in the face of setbacks, learning from constructive criticism, and seeing effort as a path to mastery. They understand that mistakes and confusion will litter the path.

Since failure is not only a part of life but also an essential part of the creative process, perhaps through carefully crafted learning experiences, we can discover "the pleasures of difficulty." In realizing that vision, explicitly teaching Wells' three levels in the thought process, normalizing difficulty through Blau's principle for fostering confusion, and nurturing the growth mindset described by Dweck offer promise.

While psychologists will probably confirm that we can't separate ego nor completely distill fear from the cognitive process, perhaps we can convey that real learning is about growth and that real growth can be uncomfortable. Learning is hard work, especially when students are urged to question, evaluate, and interpret ideas they are trying to comprehend for the first time. When engaged in these critical thinking processes, one outcome is certain: Learning can rock the core of previous knowing, causing a shift in balance. The tension between the familiar and the unfamiliar creates a wobble.

Because this invitation to change is uncomfortable, the dissonance requires management. The more that students confront challenging learning tasks to experience this dissonance, the more likely they are to befriend it as part of the learning process. When learners accept that learning is about transformation and that some discomfort is inevitable, a trip to wobble world will leave them dizzy with new wisdom and experience, not inundated by the sensation of imbalance. No longer worried about failing, learners might let go of the easy answers and find comfort in the questions.

Embracing cognitive dissonance and developing a growth mindset will be especially critical with the implementation of the Common Core State Standards (CCSS). The CCSS require students to take intellectual risks and to locate themselves in uncertainty and ambiguity. Because cognitive dissonance has unsettling effects and learning happens in stages, these changes will require time; growth will not occur without error. Even though effort doesn't guarantee outcome, this book and the strategies it shares provide a place to start.

Appendix

Annotated List of Cultural Identity Literature

American Heart by Laura Moriarty: Using tact and timing to stretch the truth and performing under the pretense that she is hitchhiking to Canada with her Aunt Chloe from Portugal, Sarah-Mary takes the reader on a journey of enlightenment. Along for the ride, readers learn some differences between Sunni and Shia Muslims, about the practice of prayer, and about what it means to have an American heart, even if you are born somewhere else.

A Night Divided by Jennifer Nielsen: Constantly under surveillance because her father Aldous Lowe was a member of the resistance, twelve-year-old Gerta feels like a disease and resents the closed-off life she is forced to live, a life of rations and restrictions, of interrogations and tortures, of prohibitions and black-market pleasures like Beatles albums and bananas. People avoid her family to prove their loyalty to the East and to stay out of prison. The Stasi—the secret police force—and the Grenzers—the border guards—cause lost friendships, broken families, and betrayals. Virtually killing self-expression, individuality, and thought, they force Germans to serve a soviet country they don't believe in.

A Tragic Kind of Wonderful by Eric Lindstorm: Through his protagonist, Lindstrom illustrates how mental illness can dislodge a person's sense of self and how it can disrupt daily life. As seventeen-year-old Mel fights for her crumbling sanity, she struggles to keep her condition secret, because for Mel, it is inconceivable to tell her friends or her therapist about her brain's stuttering and how her moods contradict reason. However, without a support system, her unbalanced self hangs in the balance. As Mel struggles to identify "which girl is the real me," she gradually discovers that she's not bipolar, although she has a bipolar disorder, and that she has to give her friends a chance to know and love the real Mel. Lindstrom's novel shares Mel's journey as she searches to define happiness, to uncover who she is, and to come to terms with her brother's death.

Bayou Magic by Jewell Parker Rhodes: Rhodes wrote this book in part to increase awareness about environmental issues and to celebrate the culture of the Louisiana bayou with its Creole cooking, swamp customs, and snappy, staccato, bouncy Zydeco music. Under Grandmère's tutelage, ten-year-old Maddy learns to call fireflies and to recognize that dreams and feelings and intuition are all ways of knowing and understanding the world. The bayou and the adventures it offers both influence and shape Maddy's identity.

Bird by Crystal Chan: A Jamaican/white/Mexican mixed-race girl living in Iowa, Jewel feels like a misfit and wonders what it would be like to have two parents who have the same languages and histories and recipes. A story with layers, *Bird* will appeal to readers interested in geology, astronomy, race, culture, and the power of human emotions. From its powerful opening line to its conclusion, Chan encourages readers to imagine beyond boundaries.

Child of the Mountains by Marilyn Sue Shank: Set in 1954 in the mountains of West Virginia where poverty is rampant, Appalachian residents value close bonds with family, friends, and neighbors and measure richness by means other than material wealth. When eleven-year-old Lydia Hawkins's brother BJ is diagnosed with cystic fibrosis and Mama agrees to participate in a research study so that BJ can receive medical treatment, the consequences of her decision leech all color from life. Through Lydia's experiences, readers realize some things are invisible until they happen to us. We might not give a second thought to prisons and prisoners until a family member is jailed; we may be blind to ignorance and hate as diseases until we are victims.

Code of Honor by Alan Gratz: A catalyst for sparking conversations on complex social issues like bullying, diversity, and the effects of prejudice, Gratz's novel uses a sports story to explore the contemporary topic of cultural collisions. Protagonist Kamran Smith, a high school senior and star running back, has dreams of going to West Point to follow in his brother Darius's footsteps as an Army Ranger. All of Kamran's dreams are destroyed when Darius is accused of being a radical Islamic terrorist and an Arizona congresswoman rescinds Kamran's letter of nomination. In the wake of Darius' acts of apparent terrorism, Kamran becomes a target for the hatred and bullying of others who call him "towel head" or "camel jockey." Because he's olive skinned and because people often care little for the facts, Kamran experiences derision and hatred.

Crossing Lines by Paul Volponi: Adonis is a starter on the school's varsity football team. Alan is the openly gay new kid, who joins the school's Fashion Club and starts cross-dressing and wearing lipstick. Before long, Alan is a pariah among certain groups and a victim of the football team's aggressive taunts and bullying. At first, Adonis goes along with the rude remarks and general belittling that the other jocks direct at Alan, particularly because he sees Alan always coming back at their behavior with his own retorts. However, Adonis' sister and girlfriend—who are friends with Alan and support his self-expression—expect Adonis to treat Alan with respect and to stand up to his teammates. When some of the jocks devise a plan to publicly humiliate and possibly hurt Alan, Adonis feels the space he's been hiding in between both sides tighten, forcing him to make the difficult choice about which lines he's willing to cross.

Do Not Pass Go by Kirkpatrick Hill: When Deet's father lands in jail for drug use, Deet's view of prisons and prisoners begins to change as Deet learns the stories of the prison inmates.

Don't Tell the Nazis by Marsha Forchuk Skrypuch: Set in 1941 in Viteretz, this historical fiction account captures events during the Soviet Occupation and subsequent German infiltration of Ukraine. Amid the horror of war and the beginnings of the Jewish Holocaust, Krystia Fediuk, a twelve-year-old girl, discovers other like-minded individuals conducting their own versions of kindness and compassion as the Ukrainians endure brutal work schedules, near starvation, and other acts of violence. Living in the midst of death, Krystia realizes that not all of the Germans are Nazis and that she has been judging them by things they cannot control. She learns to treat people as individuals and not by what she thinks or assumes about the group or nation to which that person has affiliation.

Every Single Second by Tricia Springstubb: Through Nella Sabatini, the book's twelve-year-old protagonist, readers experience how unfamiliar places often feel foreign. Although we may think the people who live in such places are not like us—with their different ideas, customs, and concerns—Nella shows readers how to navigate the cultural divide. Springstubb's book further raises social consciousness and supports unity by dispelling some of the myths and misperception about diversity. It also addresses issues of power and oppression and provides an opportunity to view these issues from a different perspective, thereby inspiring empathy building.

Faith, Hope, and Ivy June by Phyllis Reynolds Naylor: Naylor takes up the issues of crossing class lines when two girls from different parts of Kentucky participate in a student exchange program between their schools. The exchange program spotlights the role wealth and poverty play in our assumptions about one another.

Fake by Donna Cooner: Maisie Fernandez is a mixed-race girl who has been branded as one of the Froot Loops for being a high school misfit. Despite her artistic talent, sense of humor, and intelligence, she finds herself outside the hub of the magic trifecta of high school: popular, pretty, and skinny. Although Maisie has read all of the self-esteem building articles about loving the skin she's in or embracing her body size, she doesn't feel like she's enough—no matter what her mother preaches or what the self-help mantras say. On Maisie's self-discovery and self-acceptance journey, readers learn multiple lessons for living, including that we are all more than others' narrow perspectives of us and that we all have unseen hurts. In this knowledge, we can feel less isolated or alone and search out our internal securities.

Genuine Fraud by Emily Lockhart: Traumatized by her parents' deaths when she was eight years old, Jule West Williams reinvents herself with a hero origin story, a self-created person with a mysterious past who makes choices to feel stronger and more powerful. Lockhart's book is an important study of human identity, of how we often manufacture ourselves to please others and of how we are affected by the sensation of being someone else. The book essentially interrogates whether there is a true self or only a series of selves presented for different contexts.

Going Where It's Dark by Phyllis Reynolds Naylor: Thirteen-year-old Buck Anderson, whose passion is caving, is most comfortable surrounded by rock and roots and earth. Living in southwest Virginia in the Appalachian foothills, this stubborn risk-taker who craves adventure has many opportunities for discovering, exploring, and hoping to make history. Naylor, who often writes about the aspects of culture that challenge us, focuses on the roles that exceptionality and geographical circumstances play in one's life. Naylor's book also embodies an artistic expression of the differently abled experience for adolescents.

Hero-Type by Barry Lyga: Thrust into the national spotlight for stopping the attacks of a serial killer, Kross is now the focus of everyone's attention, which is almost more than he can bear. His seemingly harmless decision fuels the overarching conflict of the rest of the book. In an interesting examination of human behavior as he explores what it means to be a hero, Lyga poses some interesting questions about modern society: Do people create heroes and celebrities only so they can tear them down again? How does an individual exist in a society that has preconceived perceptions? How do we express ourselves and our beliefs in the face of the majority?

Hidden Roots by Joseph Bruchac: Through the story of twelve-year-old Howard Camp, Bruchac deconstructs stereotypes about other cultures that proliferate in the media. He also examines human mistreatment, demonstrates abuse of power by large corporations and the government, and addresses the displacement of people in the name of progress. The book further focuses on the egregious wrong of the Vermont Eugenics Project, an attempt at Native American ethnic cleansing that occurred during the first half of the twentieth century. Bruchac invites readers to respect the heritage and history of all people.

Hostage Three by Nick Lake: The Fields' life of luxury is shattered when their yacht is boarded by gun-wielding pirates who demand a hefty ransom and reduce the passengers to labels: Amy is Hostage Three. From one of their captors, Farouz, a young Somalian, Amy ironically learns about love and family loyalty. She also learns to look at life and circumstances from another perspective, one without luxury but rooted in survival, one where desperate times call for desperate measures. Once she learns Farouz's story, once she understands his motives, she grows to hate him less and less, realizing that everyone has a story.

If I Ever Get Out of Here by Eric Gansworth: Lewis Blake, who lives a complicated and lonely life, wants to be invisible when it suits him—to avoid the stares of store clerks and the whispers about wild or scary Indians from townspeople. As a "brainiac" who can speak his traditional Tuscarora language, Lewis has been tossed into junior high with twenty-two white strangers and struggles to learn their social language and to fit in. Lewis does eventually find friendship with George Haddonfield, a "military base kid" who knows what it means to be on the outside. Despite their remarkable cultural differences, the two boys discover they have a lot in common, including their love for music and The Beatles. Lewis spends the better part of junior high struggling to navigate both the white world and the reservation, wondering whether he can have an identity in both. He doesn't want to choose one to hate and one to love.

Joey Pigza Loses Control by Jack Gantos: This book makes an ideal text for a middle school unit on exceptionality. Socially, we often look upon difference as negative, as a stigma rather than as simply being different. Books about mental illness, handicapping conditions, and related issues provide opportunities to talk about the social norms that permit children to bully and tease with impunity any vulnerable "others." It allows exploration of questions like, where do we get our images of the ideal and how/why do we perpetuate them? Joey's story illustrates the destructive results that young people sometimes experience when they rely on others for acceptance and validation instead of recognizing their value themselves. The book also challenges certain assumptions about the concept of masculinity and the myth of independence.

King and the Dragonflies by Kacen Callender: This book relates the challenge that twelve-year-old Kingston Reginald James has in coping with the sudden and unexpected death of his sixteen-year-old brother Khalid. While enduring the waves of grief, King must also navigate a series of identity issues, regarding his name, gender, and the hereafter. As King comes to terms with who he really is in the wake of his brother's death, perhaps the ultimate lesson from Callender's novel is that which encourages us to learn from the dragonfly, whose 30,000 facets give it a different perspective and whose compound eyes enable it to see in all directions at the same time. Perhaps, with such sight, we wouldn't be as prone to prejudice.

King of the Screwups by K. L. Going: Starved for attention and approval and tired of competing with the professional community for his dad's love, Liam turns to drunkenness and casual sex to escape his pain. After a particularly embarrassing moment, Liam's enraged father evicts him from the house and sentences him to live with his proto-military grandparents. Unable to endure that possibility, Liam opts to live with his cross-dressing uncle, whom he calls Aunt Pete. Interested in glam, punk, rap, and metal, Pete is not afraid to stretch the boundaries. He recognizes that people are challenged when they're uncomfortable, and he finds value in that discomfort. Through the uncanny wisdom of her characters, Going teaches us all to sharpen our bullshit meters.

Of Beast and Beauty by Stacey Jay: Although the core of the story is based on the familiar *Beauty and the Beast* plot, Jay moves the conflicts beyond the traditional to warn contemporary society about the effects of intolerance and divisive philosophies and policies. Through Gem and Isra, Jay invites us all to examine our own ignorance: the darkness, the cages, the narrow worlds in which we sometimes live. She also spends immense space in defining love. Although love can feel like home, it also represents everything strange and uncertain and unknown. It means being vulnerable and beholden and embracing pain. With her two protagonists, Jay challenges people to see without the blinders of ignorance, selfishness, and elitist attitudes and to love a little harder to avoid falling into darkness.

Out of Nowhere by Maria Padian: Set in Enniston, Maine, Padian's novel features high school senior and soccer team captain Tom Bouchard. Tom's quiet hometown becomes the home to an influx of Somalian refugees who have survived a civil war and transatlantic migration only to face more conflict when certain townspeople exhibit less than hospitable reactions to their new neighbors. When the local soccer team—with the talent of its Somali teammates—begins to win and threatens to take State, additional conflict ensues. Through Tom, readers accept that life hurts and it's hard, but that unless we put aside our fury and have hope, life cannot progress positively. Inevitably life will throw curves; they'll come out of nowhere, but these challenges are best met by adapting with grace since raging only makes life harder.

Paper Daughter by Jeanette Ingold: Readers experience the Chinese Exclusion Era, a time when oppressive policies contributed to family separation, loss, and redefinition; a time when some families were formed on paper only; a time when choices prevented families from maintaining long traditions and fulfilling cultural responsibilities, thereby setting up a future shaded by doubt and guilt. The experience is not trivialized nor romanticized but treated with respect and honesty.

Party by Tom Leveen: Eleven diverse characters share varied points of view on topics that include sex, religion, the war in Iraq, and the loss of a parent. A raucous end of the year party gets busted after police are called in to stop a racially motivated fight. The book reveals that even though we share the same incident, we no doubt have a different story to tell; perspective changes the truth that a particular person sees. Readers not only discover how those differences impact reliability, they also encounter the notion of multiple truths and how sometimes we need multiple stories to determine what really happened. Ultimately, Leveen explores the human need for emotional fulfillment and understanding.

Rain Is Not My Indian Name by Cynthia Leitich Smith: After she experiences the unexpected death of her best friend, Cassidy Rain Berghoff slowly reconnects with her family and intertribal community by becoming involved as a photojournalist for her small-town newspaper. More than just the sum of her heritage—Northeastern Creek-Cherokee/Scots-Irish on her mother's side and

Irish German-Ojibway on her father's side—Rain is a unique and freethinking individual. Offering an emphasis on engineering and technology, Leitich Smith integrates the Internet in the story to make a significant plot difference.

Rule by Ellen Goodlett: Unaware of her true lineage and each hiding a traitorous secret, Zofi, Akeylah, and Florencia are summoned to Kolonya City where they learn that they are the bastard daughters of the dying King Andros. As the trio endures various tests to determine their ability to ascend to the throne, rumors swirl, people pass judgment or snub them, and a blackmailer works to sabotage the potential heirs. In the process, the girls learn that sometimes we make enemies simply for who we are. People may hate us because of our background, parentage, facial shape, or hair style. With this fantasy adventure, Goodlett exposes the dangers of exclusion and the consequences of hate. Zofi with her battle-ready stance, Ren with her steely resolve, and Akelah with her sharp intelligence teach readers not only to wear their differences with pride but to see the harm in treating people like outcasts, abusing them for sport, or denying them basic human dignity. Readers further realize that we all want our own identity, not an adjective.

Saving Red by Sonya Sones: This book written in verse lends itself to starting a conversation about mental illness and about the serious effects of anxiety and depression. Sones approaches these real but sensitive issues in a way that young adults can understand. *Saving Red* is a quick read that offers powerful, hopeful messages while remaining honest about life's not being a fairy tale. Another of the book's bonuses is what the reader can learn about Jewish cultural practices.

Shade Me by Jennifer Brown: When Peyton discovers unsavory family secrets, she moves out of Hollis Mansion, hoping to escape the unrelenting, high-pressure lifestyle of the rich and famous. Peyton ends up hospitalized, the victim of a violent assault. When Nikki Kill isn't sitting vigil at Peyton's bedside where she is reminded of her own demons, she alternates her time in the field investigating with visits to the gym, sparring and conditioning. The independent and tough main character, Nikki still looks for protection from her psychological trauma of the past. Nikki also seeks relief from the pressure that comes from her synesthesia since she knows intimately how pressure can make a person do strange things that don't engender pride.

The Art of Starving by Sam J. Miller: Sixteen-year-old Matt, who has been identified by therapists as an at-risk youth with suicidal ideation, believes he is a source of shame and embarrassment. Fixating on what makes him different—his flaming red hair, his sexual preference, his poverty, his absent father, and his alcoholic mother—Matt is mostly unaware that these differences which make him miserable might also make him a stronger, improved version of humanity. Sharing their hunger for fulfillment, their starvation for affection, attention, and validation, and their appetite for justice, young adults will likely identify with Matt's identity struggle.

The Hate U Give by Angie Thomas: After a series of devastating events, Khalil Harris, a sixteen-year-old, unarmed black boy, is shot dead by a white cop who suspected him of being a drug dealer and a thug. Starr Carter knows the truth. This novel provides a counter-narrative for those who, like Officer 115, believe that ghetto neighborhoods are poisonous, breeding nothing but low-life thugs, drug dealers, and gang bangers. Thomas encourages readers to see black lives and their circumstances from another perspective, one without luxury but rooted in survival. Once we learn Khalil's story, once we understand his motives, we realize that everyone has a story and that every life matters.

The House on Mango Street by Sandra Cisneros: All of the vignettes provide insight into Latino/Latina culture, but especially enlightening is the vignette "Those Who Don't," which shares a very human reaction to the unknown or the unfamiliar and how sometimes we draw inaccurate conclusions because of assumptions.

The Shepherd's Granddaughter by Anne Laurel Carter: About varied families, distinct economic circumstances, diverse ethnicities, experiences, home settings, regions, and lifestyles, *The Shepherd's Granddaughter* features Amani Raheem, a Palestinian girl who shares passions, ambitions, fears, values, and dilemmas familiar to most young adults. After developing an attachment to Amani's family and situation, readers cheer when Seedo recognizes the world has changed and passes his shepherd's crook, not to a son but to a granddaughter. Along with Amani, readers mourn Seedo's death, and we grow angry at the Israeli land grab, at the settler's notion of God as a real estate agent, at the injustice endured as Palestinians lose land they have worked for generations and as sheep are shot and olive groves bulldozed to ruin.

Stay by Bobbie Pyron: According to Pyron, "Everybody needs another heartbeat on their side." Told in alternating perspectives, this dog story targeted for middle-grade readers is an inspirational book about how social transformation begins with empathetic concern. By grappling with issues of social justice and fairness, Piper and her Firefly Girls Troop 423 exhibit radical courage by challenging status quo oppression with civic action.

Totally Joe by James Howe: In this realistic fiction novel, twelve-year-old Joe Bunch writes an alphabiography for his teacher Mr. Daly. As he worries about revealing details that might become ammunition used against him, Joe enlightens readers on how to live life with greater tolerance and acceptance for difference and for self rather than considering homosexuality or any other difference a perversion. The book's theme hinges on total dedication to self-esteem, development, understanding, and acceptance, while also sharing morals about civil rights and respect.

Turtles All the Way Down by John Green: Green aptly describes mental illness as an ever-tightening spiral and as the sensation of being trapped by a whirlwind of disconcerting thoughts. Aza Holmes, the novel's sixteen-year-old protagonist, lives with incapacitating anxiety and obsessive-compulsive disorder. Residing on the distant end of the spectrum, her case is not easily managed. Green's comparison to Davis Pickett's overwhelming grief regarding his absent father and the novel's insinuation that an inundation of grief is the closest that mentally typical people can come to experiencing the civil war of thought that a mentally atypical person endures promises to resonate with readers. Green also alludes to the frustration that Aza has with people who wonder if she's better/getting well. To know there are good days and bad days but no "completely well" days is a difficult concept for those who don't intimately know mental illness.

Two Boys Kissing by David Levithan: This chapterless book is a support narrative and survival story for anyone who has considered suicide or who has been ashamed of his/her body; it is a love story, and it is a book about perseverance and finding a good time in a remarkably dire place, but most of all, it is a story of hope. Although Levithan tells the tales of Tariq, Cooper, Ryan, Avery, Craig, Harry, Peter, and Neil, he also spins a tribute to all the homosexual men who came before them as forefathers in the civil rights fight. The story isn't, however, all romance and happily-ever-after. It illustrates the distinct language of a father's rage and the deeply desperate consequences of self-loathing. It explores what happens when a person loses the ability to endure and admits that we cannot kiss our way out of hell. From each of the unique stories, readers learn various secrets of strength, acceptance, and beauty. Most of all, Levithan celebrates life and love as the ultimate gifts.

Up to This Pointe by Jennifer Longo: High school senior Harper doesn't belong to the discourse community of scientists. The language she knows especially well is that spoken by ballet dancers: pointe shoes, rond de jambe turns, grand jetés, battements, and pliés. But under the influence of the geography and the beauty of Antarctica, Harper falls in love with the Adélie penguins and learns to think in questions. Longo's book invites readers to engage with the characters, to experience "a truth informed by facts, but not made up entirely of them" (Longo, Author's Note), and to explore the question: What would I do if this were happening to me?

We Set the Dark on Fire and *We Unleash the Merciless Storm* by Tehlor Kay Mejia: These books are duology that follows the lives of Carmen Santos and Daniela Vargas, two La Voz freedom fighters who hope to undermine systemic prejudice. In the upper-class society of Medio, the power structure prioritizes the wealthy and leaves the rest to suffer. Although the wealthy share a narrative about privilege and destiny, the real story is about greed and money and politics and privilege and prejudice. The real story is that humans live in a system that was created thousands of years ago by people who wanted to reward those like them and punish everyone else. Like many other good stories, this one doesn't have a fairy tale ending, although it does have an emotionally satisfying one as Mejia skillfully balances issues like class, gender, and immigration with a gripping love story.

OTHER IDEAS FOR HONORING IDENTITY

Another resource for book titles that support place are state literary maps. A literary map is a map that acknowledges the contributions of authors to a specific state or region. Many states maintain literary maps that highlight their area's literary heritage. The Library of Congress, with its Center for the Book project, has an affiliate in each of the fifty states. Consulting any state's Center for the Book will enable individuals to discover what takes place in their home states or find materials for supporting literacy.

Commonlit.org is an additional resource (https://www.commonlit.org/). From this useful website, teachers can access instructional materials that support literacy development for students in grades 3–12. For example, the "Choose a Lesson" tool enables educators to search the organization's collection of fiction and nonfiction and filter by Lexile measure, grade, theme, genre, literary device, or common core standard.

References

Adams, M., Bell, L. A., & Griffin, P. (1997). *Teaching for diversity and social justice: A sourcebook.* New York: Routledge.

Adichie, C. N. (2009, July). The danger of a single story. [Video file]. Retrieved from www.ted.com/talks/chimamanda_adichie_the_danger_of_a_single_story.

Adolescent literacy: A policy research brief. (2007). National Council of Teachers of English. James R. Squire Office for Policy Research [PDF file]. Retrieved from https://secure.ncte.org/library/NCTEFiles/Resources/Positions/Chron0907ResearchBrief.pdf.

Alexie, S. (2007). *The absolutely true diary of a part-time Indian.* New York: Little, Brown.

Anti-Defamation League. (2005). *Pyramid of hate* [PDF file]. Retrieved from https://www.adl.org/sites/default/files/.../pdf/.../Pyramid-of-Hate.pdf.

Applebee, A. (1996). *Curriculum as conversation: Transforming traditions of teaching and learning.* Chicago: University of Chicago Press.

Applebee, A., Langer, J. A., Nystrand, M., & Gamoran, A. (Fall 2003). Discussion-based approaches to developing understanding: Classroom instruction and student performance in middle and high school English. *American Educational Research Journal,* 40(3), 685–730.

Appleman, D. (2009). *Critical encounters in high school English* (2nd ed.). New York: Teachers College Press.

Bakhtin, M. M. (1981). *The dialogic imagination: Four essays.* Austin: University of Texas Press.

Baldwin, J. (2010). *The cross of redemption: Uncollected writings.* R. Keenan (Ed.). New York: Random House.

Bandura, A. (1997). *Self-efficacy: The exercise of control.* New York: Longman.

Banks, J. A. (2010). Multicultural education: Characteristics and goals. In J. A. Banks & C. A. McGee Banks (Eds.), *Multicultural education: Issues and perspectives* (7th ed., pp. 3–26). Hoboken: John Wiley and Sons.

Becker, K. M., Pehrsson, D. E., & McMillen, P. S. (2008). Bibliolinking: An adaption of bibliotherapy for university students in transition. *Journal of Poetry Therapy*, 21(4), 231–35.

Bennett, J. (2009, November 2). *Tamara's opus* [Video file]. Retrieved from www.youtube.com/watch?v=_U5BwD8zOeM.

Bishop, R. S. (1990). Mirrors, windows, and sliding glass doors. *Perspectives*, 6(3), ix–xi.

Blau S. (2003). *The literature workshop: Teaching texts and their readers*. Portsmouth, NH: Heinemann.

Blume, J. (n.d.). Judy Blume talks about censorship. Retrieved from http://judyblume.com/censorship.php.

Böckler, A., Herrmann, L., Trautwein, F. M. et al. (June 2017). Know thy selves: Learning to understand oneself increases the ability to understand others. *Journal of Cognitive Enhancement*, 1(2), 197–209. https://doi.org/10.1007/s41465-017-0023-6.

Bouchard, D. (1995). *If you're not from the prairie . . . .* New York: Aladdin Paperbacks.

Bradbury, R. (1951). *The illustrated man*. New York: Bantam Books.

Bradby, M. (2000). *Momma, where are you from?* New York: Scholastic.

Brandt, D. (2001). *Literacy in American lives*. New York: Cambridge University Press.

Bronfenbrenner, U. (1979). *The ecology of human development*. Cambridge: Harvard University Press.

Bruchac, J. (2004). *Hidden roots*. New York: Scholastic.

Bucher, K. T., & Hinton, K. M. (2013). *Young adult literature: Exploration, evaluation, and appreciation* (3rd ed.). Upper Saddle River, NJ: Pearson.

Buleen, Chad. (2020, January 3). Crazy Horse memorial facts. Retrieved from https://traveltips.usatoday.com/crazy-horse-memorial-62985.html.

Carvell, M. (2005). *Sweetgrass basket*. New York: Dutton Children's Books.

Castagno, A. E., & Brayboy, B. M. J. 2008, December. Culturally responsive schooling for indigenous youth: A review of the literature. *Review of Educational Research*, 78(4), 941–93.

Center for Communication and Civic Engagement. (2013). Culture jamming. Retrieved from http://ccce.com.washington.edu/.

Chenoweth, E. (2016, June 23). Majority rule/Minority rights: Essential principles. Retrieved from democracyweb.org/majority-rule-principles.

Cohen, M. (2006). *First grade takes a test*. New York: Starlight Books.

Collins, S. (2009). *Catching fire*. New York: Scholastic.

Common Core State Standards Initiative. (2018). English Language Arts Standards » Anchor Standards » College and Career Readiness Anchor Standards for Reading. Retrieved from http://www.corestandards.org/ELA-Literacy/CCRA/R/.

Cowley, G. (June 1996). The biology of beauty. *Newsweek*, 127(23), 61–66.

Clifton, L. (1987). *Good woman: Poems and a memoir 1969–1980*. Rochester: BOA Editions, Ltd.

Cuddy, A. (2012, October). Your body language shapes who you are. [Video file]. Retrieved from www.ted.com/talks/amy_cuddy_your_body_language_may_shape_who_you_are.

Davis, A. (Ed.). (2012). *Taking action: Readings for civic reflection.* Chicago: The Great Books Foundation.

Delpit, L. (2012). *"Multiplication is for white people": Raising expectations for other people's children.* New York: New Press.

———. (1995). *Other people's children.* New York: Free Press.

Dewey J. (1910). *How we think.* Boston, MA: D.C. Heath.

Dewey J. (1938). *Experience and education.* New York: Simon & Schuster.

Douglas, W. O. (1953, January). The one un-American act. *Nieman Reports,* 7(1), 20.

Dweck, C. S. (2010, September). Even geniuses work hard. *Educational Leadership,* 68(1), 16–20.

———. (2007–2008, December/January). The secret to raising smart kids. *Scientific American Mind,* 18(6), 36–43.

———. (1986). "Motivational processes affecting learning." *American Psychologist,* 41, 1040–48.

Earling, D. M. (July, 2003). *We connect through stories.* Presentation at Montana Writing Project Summer Institute, Missoula, MT. Ellis, K. N. (2003). "Raised by women." Tougaloo Blues. Chicago: Third World Press.

Ellis, K. N. (2003). *"Raised by women." Tougaloo Blues.* Chicago: Third World Press.

Erickson, F. (2010). Culture in society and in educational practices. In J. A. Banks & C. A. McGee Banks (Eds.), *Multicultural education: Issues and perspectives* (7th ed., pp. 33–53). Hoboken: John Wiley and Sons.

Fein, H. (1979). *Accounting for genocide: National responses and Jewish victimization during the Holocaust.* New York: Free Press.

Fleischman, P. (1997). *Seedfolks.* New York: Joanna Colter Books.

Forster, E. M. (1927). *Aspects of the novel.* New York: Harcourt, Inc.

Gaitan, C. D. (2006). *Building culturally responsible classrooms: A guide for K–6 teachers.* Thousand Oaks, CA: Corwin Press.

Gallo, D. R. (2008, January). "Bold books for teenagers." *English Journal,* 97(3), 114–17.

Gansworth, E. (2013). *If I ever get out of here.* New York: Arthur A. Levine Books.

Gardner, H. (2008). *Five minds for the future* (2nd ed.). Boston: Harvard Business Press.

———. (1983). *Frames of mind: The theory of multiple intelligences.* New York: Basic Books, Inc.

Gay, G. (2000). *Culturally responsive teaching: theory, research, and practice.* New York: Teachers College Press.

Gee, J. (1989). Literacy, discourse, and linguistics: Introduction and what is literacy? *Journal of Education,* 171(1), 5–25.

Going, K. L. (2009). *King of the screwups.* Boston: Harcourt.

Gopalakrishnan, A. (2011). *Multicultural children's literature: A critical issues approach.* Thousand Oaks, CA: SAGE Publications.

Hall, M. P. (2013). The four idols of Francis Bacon and the new instrument of knowledge. Retrieved from http://www.sirbacon.org/links/4idols.htm.

Halsted, J. W. (1994). *Some of my best friends are books.* Columbus: Ohio Psychology Press.

Heider, F. (1958). *The psychology of interpersonal relations.* New York: Wiley.

Henrix, Jimi. (2010). Music: Jimi Hendrix quotes. Retrieved from http://www.Goodquotes.com.

Hoagland, T. (2003). *What narcissism means to me.* St. Paul: Graywolf Press.

Jensen, E. (2009). *Teaching with poverty in mind: What being poor does to kids' brains and what schools can do about it.* Alexandria, VA: ASCD.

Kagan, J. (1972). Motives and development. *Journal of Personality and Social Psychology*, 22(1), 51–66.

Kappelman, T. (2002, July 14). Marshall McLuhan: "The medium is the message." Probe Ministries. Retrieved from www.leaderu.com/orgs/probe/docs/mcluhan.html.

Kaufman, G. (1996). *Psychology of shame: Theory and treatment of shame-based syndromes* (2nd ed.). New York: Springer Publishing Company.

Latrobe, K. H., & Drury, J. (2009). *Critical approaches to young adult literature.* New York: Neal Shuman.

Livio, M. (2005). *The equation that couldn't be solved.* New York: Simon & Schuster.

Longo, J. (2016). *Up to this pointe.* New York: Random House Books for Young Readers.

Lutz, C. E. (1978). The oldest library motto: ψγxhσ Iatpeion. *The Library Quarterly*, 48(1), 36–39.

Lyga, B. (2008). *Hero-type.* New York: Houghton Mifflin.

Marzano, R. (2010). Teaching inference. *Educational Leadership*, 67(7), 80–81.

McCloud, C. (2007). *Have you filled a bucket today?* Northville, MI: Ferne Press.

McDonald, M. (1996). *My house has stars.* New York: Orchard Books.

McNeil, J. (1999). *Curriculum: The teacher's initiative* (2nd ed.). Upper Saddle River, NJ: Merrill.

Mead, M. (2003). *Studying contemporary western society: Method and theory.* New York: Berghahn Books.

Metzger, K., Box, A., & Blasingame, J. (2013). Embracing intercultural diversification: Teaching young adult literature with Native American themes. *English Journal*, 102(5), 57–62.

Michaels, S., O'Connor, C., & Resnick, L. (2008). Deliberative discourse idealized and realized: Accountable talk in the classroom and in civic life. *Studies in Philosophy and Education*, 27, 283–97.

Miller, D. L. (2014, Summer). Building bridges with cultural identity literature. *The ALAN Review*, 41(3), 31–38.

———. (2013, February). Got it wrong? Think again. And again. *Phi Delta Kappan*, 94(5), 50–52.

———. (2012, Summer). Tough talk as an antidote to bullying. *English Journal*, 101(6), 30–36.

———. (2012, Summer). The healing power of art. *The ALAN Review*, 39(3), 30–35.

Moll, L., et al. (1992). Funds of knowledge for teaching: Using a qualitative approach to connect homes and classrooms. *Theory into Practice*, 31(2), 132–41.

Montana Office of Public Instruction. (2011, November). Montana Common Core Standards. *English Language Arts and Literacy in History/Social Studies, Science, and Technical Subjects* [PDF]. Retrieved from https://opi.mt.gov/Educators/Teaching-Learning/K-12-Content-Standards-Revision/English-Language-Arts-Literacy-Standards.

Newkirk, T. (2012). *The art of slow reading.* Portsmouth, NH: Heinemann.

Nin, A. (1961). *Seduction of the minotaur.* Chicago: Swallow Press.

Nussbaum, M. C. (2010). *Not for profit: Why democracy needs the humanities.* Princeton: Princeton University Press.

——. (1996). *Cultivating humanity: A classical defense of reform in liberal education.* Cambridge: Harvard University Press.

Nye, N. S. (2008). *Honeybee.* New York: Greenwillow Books.

——. (2002). *19 varieties of gazelle: Poems of the Middle East.* New York: Greenwillow Books.

O'Donnell-Allen, C. (2011). *Tough talk, tough texts.* Portsmouth, NH: Heinemann.

Ormrod, J. E. (2008). *Educational psychology* (6th ed.). Upper Saddle River, NJ: Pearson.

Palmer, P. (2007). *The courage to teach* (10th anniversary ed.). San Francisco: Jossey-Bass.

Paul Klee: Paintings, Biography and Quotes. (2009). Retrieved from www.paulklee.net/.

Peterson, R., & Eeds, M. (2007). *Grand conversations: Literature groups in action.* New York: Scholastic.

Racism against Somalis cited in Minn. school brawl. (2013, February 15). *USA Today.* Retrieved from www.usatoday.com/story/news/nation/2013/02/15/minneapolis-high-school-food-fight/1923547/.

Ray, K. W. (1999). *Wondrous words.* Urbana, IL: NCTE.

Rasinski, T. V., & Padak, N. D. (1990). Multicultural learning through children's literature. *Language Arts*, 67(6), 576–80.

Richardson, J., & Parnell, P. (2005). *And tango makes three.* New York: Simon & Shuster.

Robert Frost Quotes. (n.d.). BrainyQuote.com. Retrieved from https://www.brainyquote.com/quotes/robert_frost_101423.

Robert Frost Quotes. (n.d.). Pass It On.com. Retrieved October 25, 2011 from https://www.passiton.com/inspirational-quotes/3477-education-is-the-ability-to-listen-to-almost

Roiphe, A. (1988). *A season for healing: Reflections on the holocaust.* New York: Summit Books.

Romano, T. (2008). *Zigzag: A life of reading and writing, teaching and learning.* Portsmouth, NH: Heinemann.

Rylant, C. (1982). *When I was young in the mountains.* New York: Puffin Books.

Sendak, M. (1993). *We are all in the dumps with jack and guy.* New York: HarperCollins.

Sewell, A. (1911). *Black beauty: The autobiography of a horse.* New York: Barse & Hopkins.

Shechtman, Z. (2009). *Treating child and adolescent aggression through bibliotherapy.* New York: Springer Publishing Company.

Shulman, L. S. (1997). Disciplines of inquiry in education: A new overview. In R. M. Jaeger (Ed.), *Contemporary methods for research in education* (2nd ed., pp. 3–28). Washington, D.C.: American Education Research Association.

Stanbrough, R. J., García, M. J., & King, L. (2020, January). Position statement on indigenous peoples and people of color in English and language arts materials. Retrieved from https://ncte.org/statement/ipoc/.

Steinem, G. (2009). In defense of the "chick flick." In P. Eschholz, A. Rosa, & V. Clark (Eds.), *Language awareness: Readings for college writers* (10th ed., pp. 302–04). Boston: Bedford/St. Martin's.

Street, B. (2001). "The new literacy studies." In E. Cushman, E. R. Kintgen, B. Kroll, & M. Rose (Eds.) *Literacy: A Critical Sourcebook* (pp. 430–66). Boston: Bedford/St. Martin's.

———. (1995). *Social literacies: Critical approaches to literacy in development, ethnography, and education.* London: Longman.

Tiger Lily: How To Grow & Care For *Lilium Lancifolium* (2019, January 2). Retrieved from https://www.epicgardening.com/tiger-lily/.

United States Holocaust Memorial Museum. (2012). Martin Niemöller. In *Holocaust Encyclopedia.* https://encyclopedia.ushmm.org/content/en/article/martin-niemoeller-first-they-came-for-the-socialists.

Vygotsky, L. (1978). *Mind in society: The development of higher psychological processes.* Cambridge: Harvard University Press.

Watsky, G. (2010, April 18). S for lisp. [Video file]. Retrieved from www.youtube.com/watch?v=6GvTLfV8fls.

Weiner, B. (1985, October). An attributional theory of achievement motivation and emotion. *Psychological Review*, 92(4), 548–73.

Wells, K. (2009, April). Learning and teaching critical thinking: From a Peircean perspective. *Educational Philosophy and Theory*, 41(2), 201–18.

Young, A. L. (2011). LGBT students want educators to speak up for them. *Kappan*, 93(2), 35–37.

Zitlow, C. S., & Stover, L. T. (2011, Winter). Portrait of the artist as a young adult: Who is the real me? *The ALAN Review*, 32–42.

Index

accommodations, 37, 133
accountable talk levels, 25, 76, 83
action continuum, 78, 128
Adbusters.org, 79
agency, student or youth, ix, 22, 64–65, 79
Alexie, Sherman, 31, 32, 60
ally behavior, 50, 51, 54, 110, 131
argument literacy, 58, 61, 79–82, 86–89, 102, 106, 107, 134
art, influence and transformative power of, 13–14, 21–26, 32–34
attributional retraining, 39–40, 124, 133–135

Bandura, Alfred, 42
Banksy, 79, 80
Banned Books Week, 82, 90–92
beautylust, 105
bias, 8, 9, 13, 49, 52–53, 104, 108, 109, 127,
bibliotherapy, 123, 124, 126
binary thinking, 54, 77, 103, 125, 126–127
bio-poem, 17–18, 26–27
Blau, Sheridan, 137, 138
bold books. *See* provocative texts
Brandt, Deborah, 11
Bronfenbrenner, Urie, 129, 130, 131

bullying, 59, 60, 78, 84, 95, 98, 110, 128, 131, 142, 143, 146
Busy Intersection Method, 52, 78

CEO strategy, 50–51, 78, 114–115
civil discourse, ix, 4, 13, 25, 58, 102, 107, 108
cognitive disequilibrium, 128, 129, 136–139
Collins, Suzanne, 23–24, 60
Common Core State Standards, 63, 102, 111, 123, 139, 151
consensual decision making, 77
critical thinking, xi, 12, 22–25, 52, 57, 58, 77, 79, 80, 81, 82, 83, 86–89, 102–104, 106, 108, 111, 114, 128, 129, 132, 136–139
cross-cultural comprehension, 5, 9, 94, 97–103, 107–108, 116, 126
Cuddy, Amy, 40
cultural broker, teacher as, 11
Cultural Identity Literature, vii–viii, ix, xi, 4, 5, 12, 22–23, 25, 59, 93–117, 129, 132, 133, 141–151
cultural lens, 1, 9–10, 12, 52, 116, 125
culturally responsive mindset, 12, 52, 108, 116
culturally responsive teaching/schooling, vii, viii, ix, 2, 4, 8, 12, 18, 35, 55

culture, vii, viii, 3–4, 8–11, 18, 51, 54–58, 88, 94, 95, 97
culture jamming, 80

Delpit, Lisa, 8–9, 36
Dewey, John, 127, 136
dialogic exchange, xi, 4–5, 12, 57, 75–83, 102, 106–107, 111, 116
dialogue pedagogy, 12–13, 75–79, 82, 121, 124, 128, 134
discourse community(ies), 8, 10, 35, 44, 65, 101, 114, 121, 150
doubt management, 12, 82, 102, 105, 129, 136–137
Dweck, Carol, 43, 138

empathy, empathy building, ix, 4, 9, 12, 21–22, 51, 94, 95, 97, 107–108, 117, 123

failure as part of the learning process, 20, 38, 39, 40, 65, 135–136, 138
find the star, 63
funds of knowledge, 36, 62

Gallo, Don, 59
Gardner, Howard, 22
Gee, James, 44
GREEN APPLE acronym, vii–ix, 2–4, 8, 10, 12–13, 94, 99–101, 103, 106, 108, 111–113, 116, 117, 119–121, 125, 126
growth mindset, 19, 38, 138, 139

idols, 8
inferences/inferencing, 13, 46, 123, 124, 127

Klee, Paul, 47, 58

literature circles, 111
Longo, Jennifer, 113–115, 150–151

McLuhan, Marshal, 57–58

metacognition, 9, 11, 19, 31, 44–46, 52, 57, 63, 77, 80, 96, 102, 107, 124, 128, 133, 136
modifications, 37
multicultural literacy, 1, 2, 10–11, 93–94
multi-genre memoir, 17–18

National Council of Teachers of English (NCTE), 2, 94, 97
National Writing Project, xi, 17,
Nin, Anais, 8
normalizing confusion, 136–139
normalizing difference, 102–103, 105
Nussbaum, Martha, 21, 22, 117
Nye, Naomi Shihab, 21, 25

pause and ponder moments, 5, 45, 123–128, 133
power-posing, 40–42, 44
preservice teachers, 18, 19, 57, 108, 133
productive persistence, 19, 20, 38, 39
provocative texts, 7, 13, 23–24, 25, 32–34, 44, 55, 56–57, 58, 59, 60–61, 62, 76, 77, 78, 79, 80, 81, 83–86, 89–92, 95–97, 102, 103, 107–110, 113–115, 126, 128, 132
psychological schema, 7, 102, 104–105, 113, 114, 115, 117
psychological scripts, 7, 104–106, 117
Pyramid of Hate, 109–110, 131

rationale, 95, 96–97, 118–119
Ray, Katie Wood, 27
reflection. *See* metacognition
reowning, 125
Romano, Tom, 17

scaffold, 37, 43, 56, 61, 75–76, 112, 137
semiotics, 88, 89, 115–116, 125
self-efficacy, 42–44
sharing circle, 16, 51

social justice, ix, 1, 3, 4, 11, 12–13, 21, 24–25, 49–66. 77, 79, 100, 126, 128, 131, 132, 149
subvertising, 80
suspended conclusion, 127, 136, 137

taking a line for a walk, 47, 58
tetrad, 57–58
think abouts, 44–47, 107
three-tier approach, 50
tough topics. *See* provocative texts

uncertainty resolution, 105, 128–129, 137
universe of obligation, 129–131

Vygotsky, Lev, 124, 128, 129

warm demander, 36–37, 43
Writer's Notebook, 44–47, 85

Zone of Proximal Development, 128

About the Author

Donna L. Miller, PhD, is an adjunct instructor, educational consultant, co-director of Writing Projects Under the Big Sky, and manager of www.thinkingzone.org. She has taught in the secondary school system for twenty-six years, as well as in several teacher training programs, serving as director for five years. Her research interests revolve around young adult literature and issues of literacy sponsorship.

www.ingramcontent.com/pod-product-compliance
Lightning Source LLC
Chambersburg PA
CBHW020740230426
43665CB00009B/500